MONEY, POWER,

FAME IN ASTROLOGY

Au Yong Chee Tuck

For book orders, email orders@traffordpublishing.com.sg

Most Trafford Singapore titles are also available at major online book retailers.

Printed in Singapore.

ISBN: 978-1-4669-3137-4 (sc)
ISBN: 978-1-4669-3138-1 (hc)
ISBN: 978-1-4669-3139-8 (e)

Trafford rev. 11/26/2012

 www.traffordpublishing.com.sg

Singapore
toll-free: 800 101 2656 (Singapore)
Fax: 800 101 2656 (Singapore)

CONTENTS

DEDICATED TO:

MASTER FRANCIS LEYAU YOKE SAI
FOR SHOWING HIS STUDENTS *"THE WAY"*

ACKNOWLEDGEMENTS

This book would not have seen the light of the day if it had not been for the helpful staff at Trafford Publishing, Singapore.

In particular, we wish to thank Jem Adams for her encouragement and Sydney Felicio for her invaluable assistance.

The other acknowledgements will be made in the course of our articles. It seemed cumbersome and out of context to mention them here. It would not have been possible for us to do our work if it had not been for the painstaking and original research done by the journalists, historians and writers who came before us.

"THE TIME HAS COME TO TALK OF MANY THINGS . . ."

"The time has come," the Walrus said,
"To talk of many things:
Of shoes—and ships—and sealing-wax—
Of cabbages—and kings—
And why the sea is boiling hot—
And whether pigs have wings."

(from Lewis Carroll's "Through the Looking Glass and what Alice found there," 1872)

*W*elcome to *"Money, Power, Fame in Astrology."* Why choose such an odd title for our work?

The themes of money, power, fame (and love) are universal in humanity, regardless of race, or religion, class or caste. Any practicing astrologer would find that these are the most common issues raised by the clients. Whether we examine the lives of the rich or the poor, the powerful or the ordinary, the famous or the unknown, these topics crop up again and again.

The first person in our galaxy of characters is the musician who had it all—money, fame, women. The only thing missing in Xavier Cugat's life was children. Despite marrying five wives, none of them bore him any children.

The next pair of persons we shall encounter were two actresses who shared a common element at birth. Both Anne Bancroft and

Shirley MacLaine were born on a wood element day. The difference was that the former was a weak wood person while the latter was a strong wood person. This factor influenced them to become entirely different characters. MacLaine became too superstitious and too involved about the supernatural and occult matters. Both had successful careers but they worked together professionally only once, in the 1977 movie "The Turning Point."

The most powerful person in Europe in the 1930s was Adolf Hitler. He also had the wood element in his birth chart. In fact, since he was born in spring, his wood element was at peak strength. In the study of Chinese astrology, wood is supposed to represent kindness and benevolence. But surely no historian or even layman would care to consider Hitler as kind in any way, certainly not after the Holocaust and the Final Solution.

In November 1974, an unknown paleontologist excavating in Ethiopia was a very worried man. His funds which were meant for two years were rapidly running out by the end of the first year. He had to find something worthwhile and find it fast. In the event, Donald Carl Johanson found the fossils he later named "Lucy". Was it chance or human choice that led him to the find of his lifetime?

Many purists who studied astrology scoff at incomplete birth charts. They argued that the birth chart must be complete with the hour of birth in order to give a meaningful analysis. There are merits in their arguments. We have presented an ideal birth chart, complete with birth hour of twin brothers. But there is a dearth of biographical data about Peter and Anthony Shaffer. How does one begin his analysis if there are no biographical details? We do not live in an ideal world after all. The perfect birth chart is of limited use if there is insufficient biographical information.

Why do we need such information? Surely any competent astrologer should be able to make an analysis based on the birth chart alone. That may be so but it ignored the human factor of choice in destiny reading. For instance, the astrologer could deduce whether the marriage would work out or end in disaster. But the astrologer could *not* tell from the chart whether or not the subject *chose* to marry, to divorce or to remarry.

In 1964, a struggling film director in Italy shot a spaghetti Western with an unknown American actor in the lead role. The result was "A Fistful of Dollars" which would launch the careers of Sergio Leone and Clint Eastwood. But Sergio Leone did not have any fire element in his birth chart. Some astrology masters argued that one must have both the fire and the water elements in his birth chart in order to have any potential for achievement in life. Their reasoning was that fire and water were polarities and both were essential to sustain life. If this were so, how did one explain the success of Sergio Leone?

To some people, fame was an integral part of success. People involved in arts and entertainment, politics and sports needed fame and authority in order to succeed in their careers. A singer or actor who was famous could command a higher fee or royalty from the studio. The footballer or athlete who was well known would be asked to endorse the products from the sports equipment companies. The politician who had authority would have a more effective voice whether in government or in opposition.

One obscure man who found fame to be a burden was Thomas Edward Lawrence. When he became known as "Lawrence of Arabia", he used his fame to plead for the Arab cause of self-governance in Syria in the decade after the end of the First World War. After this objective was achieved, he wanted to fade into obscurity. But the media refused to forget him and followed his military career with interest. Why did fame turn out to be such a drag instead of an asset?

After the defeat of Japan in August 1945 ended the Second World War, the people in Vietnam were dismayed when the French returned to reclaim their colonial empire. One frail old man with a wispy beard stood in the way. He turned to the Americans for assistance in their struggle for independence against the French. Initially, the Truman Administration seemed sympathetic.

Later they realized that they did not want to antagonize a former war time ally. They were also wary about supporting what they perceived to be a potential Communist threat. This infuriated the old man with the wispy beard who then turned to China and the Soviet Union for help. The Americans would have cause enough to remember his name—Ho Chi Minh. He predicted that "the tiger would maul the elephant." Whose power would prevail? How could the iron will of one former peasant ever prevail against two Western powers who commanded vast technological and industrial resources?

In the early 1970s, a promising young actress was given a lead role as "Princess Leia" in what became the first trilogy of the "Star Wars" movies. It could have been the start of a lucrative acting career. Instead, Carrie Fisher descended into the world of drugs. She eventually went into drug rehabilitation and wrote several novels about her experiences. These books sold well enough to establish her second career as a writer. Why did someone who had such a promising start throw it all away? Was it Fate or human choice?

In 1957, a promising French writer became the second youngest person to receive the Nobel Prize for Literature. Yet winning the Prize did not seem to bring him success and contentment. Instead, Albert Camus was vilified by both the French government and the Algerians for his views about the Algerian War for Independence. In the event, he did not live long enough to see the conclusion of the Algerian War in 1962. Within three years of winning the Prize, he was killed in an automobile accident.

He did not have a single spark of fire in his birth chart. Here we have to return to the theme of the polarities of fire and water. How did someone whose chart was so wet and cold ever hope to have any achievement in life?

Some writers who have won the Nobel Prize are largely forgotten today. Mention the names Par Lagerkvist, Halldor Laxness and Ivo Andric to the reading public. The chances are that the average reader cannot easily name a single work by any one of them. Yet these writers won the Nobel Prize for Literature in 1951, 1955 and 1961 respectively—that is, the years immediately before and after Albert Camus accepted his Prize in 1957. But unlike the other winners, the works of Albert Camus are still available in print today and continued to be read—not only in French but in translation to other major languages—even decades after his death. This proved that his success was real and permanent, not transitory and dependent on the Prize alone.

If Albert Camus wrote "serious" novels and essays, another writer who found success writing popular fiction was the creator of "James Bond." Ian Fleming lived the dissolute lifestyle of a philanderer, addicted to his nicotine and his liquor. Inevitably, he would imbibe his hero with similar characteristics in the fourteen books that he wrote. If he had created a hero who was more chaste and inconspicuous, the public would probably not have found such a humdrum spy appealing. But Ian Fleming drove himself to an early grave in 1964 by his heavy smoking and drinking.

In August 1967, one immigrant Chinese American decided to turn his company, Wang Laboratories, public. Then he brought his son, Fred Wang, into the company as head of research in October 1983. The senior management argued that the son had no ability to manage a large public listed company. But the father was getting old and wanted to leave a legacy. He refused to listen and installed his son as president in November 1986. The three design chiefs and the head of the sales division mutinied by resigning. When the company's performance deteriorated further, the father was compelled to dismiss his son in August 1989. It was the last corporate decision that An Wang would ever make. By March 1990, he died a broken hearted man.

We began our work by exploring the theme of children. Perhaps it was only fitting that we should conclude by returning to this theme in our last article.

BEFORE WE BEGIN—OR THE LEAST
YOU NEED TO KNOW

If the reader is not familiar with Chinese astrology, here is a brief introduction. In the study of Chinese astrology, there is the concept of Yin and Yang. Examples of Yin could be feminine, dark, cold, soft, yielding, and supple. Examples of Yang might include male, light, warmth. The underlying theme is that Yin and Yang must exist together, that is, they are complementary. Although they might appear to be opposites such as light and darkness, we should bear in mind that if there is light, then there should be shadow. The shadow cannot exist without the light and the light will inevitably cause a shadow. Professional artists and photographers usually have a good understanding of light and shadow. Indeed, it is their play with light and shadow, among other things, that makes them outstanding artists.

There is also the concept of the five elements which are wood, fire, earth, metal and water. These elements do not exist in isolation. There are three cycles that link the five elements in a meaningful way—the production cycle, the controlling cycle and the weakening cycle.

Wood provided the fuel for fire, therefore wood produces fire. When fire burns up the wood, the result is ashes or earth. Fire is said to produce earth. The earth buries the metal and when the earth is excavated, the minerals can be found. In that sense, earth produces metal. When the metal rod is heated at high temperatures, it will melt and liquefy. So metal is said to produce water. These processes form the production cycle.

In the controlling cycle, the roots of the tree grip the earth. Wood is said to control earth. Earth determines the direction and flow of water such as in the case of the banks of a river. Thus, earth controls water. Water puts out fire so water controls fire. As fire melts metal, fire is said to control metal. A metal axe or saw can chop down a tree. The metal is said to control the wood.

In the weakening cycle, wood absorbs water from the soil. So wood weakens water. If metal is exposed to water for prolonged periods, the water can corrode the metal or cause the metal to rust. Water is said to weaken metal. Too much metal buried under the earth exhausts the earth. Thus it is said that metal weakens the earth. If there is excessive earth, it will dim the fire. Therefore, earth weakens the fire. But earth did not entirely put out the fire. Water is required to put out the fire, not earth. That is the difference between the weakening cycle and the controlling cycle.

When we match the concept of Yin and Yang to the concept of the Five Elements, we get the ten Heavenly Stems. That is, each of the five elements has a Yin and Yang side to it. The ten Heavenly Stems are Yang Wood, Yin Wood, Yang Fire, Yin Fire, Yang Earth, Yin Earth, Yang Metal, Yin Metal, Yang Water and Yin Water. Readers who are discerning may have noticed that the ten Heavenly Stems follow the pattern of the production cycle.

Then there are the twelve animals or what is technically known as the Earthly Branches. The twelve animals, in order of appearance are Rat, Ox, Tiger, Rabbit, Dragon, Snake, Horse, Goat, Monkey, Rooster, Dog and Pig. In compiling an astrological chart, it is the practice to write the Heavenly Stem above the Earthly Branch.

That brief summary has just about covered the basics of Chinese astrology, hopefully sufficient for the reader to follow some of the arguments in the articles that follow.

CHAPTER ONE

HE HAD EVERYTHING IN LIFE—EXCEPT CHILDREN

"Rhumba is my Life"
(Xavier Cugat, circa 1948)

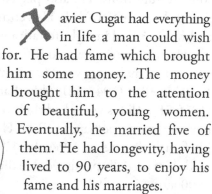

Xavier Cugat had everything in life a man could wish for. He had fame which brought him some money. The money brought him to the attention of beautiful, young women. Eventually, he married five of them. He had longevity, having lived to 90 years, to enjoy his fame and his marriages.

Yet something seemed to be missing in his life. He had no children. Despite five marriages, three of them lengthy, he remained childless to the end of his days. His last marriage ended when he was 78 years old. This effectively meant that for the last 12 years of his life, he had no wife or children to care for him. Despite all his material success, he could not have children. Were the Fates kind or cruel to him?

Xavier Cugat was born at the turn of the century on 1 January 1900 in Barcelona. His parents were political refugees who fled to Havana, Cuba when he was aged three or five. It was said that he was given a violin at the age of four and when he was 10 he played with an orchestra, becoming first violinist two years later. When Enrico Caruso visited Havana, he was impressed with his playing. Caruso brought Cugat with him on his planned tour of South America.

But Cugat was not enamoured of the violin. He did not want to remain a violinist all his life. He found that he could also draw. In 1924, he found a job with the *"Los Angeles Times"* as a cartoonist. He also found work in the movie business due to his fame as the band leader that played Latin American music. He had established a reputation as the "Rhumba King" for popularising tangos, mumbas and cha-chas. By the 1930s, he began to appear with his band in some feature films. He also played in hotels such as the Waldorf Astoria hotel in New York. He ventured into the restaurant business and was involved in eight restaurants.

His first marriage was to Rita Montaner in 1918 until 1920. His subsequent marriages were to Carmen Elen Castillo (1929-1940), Lorraine Allen (1947-52), Abbe Lane (1952-64) and Charro Baeza (1966-78). All his wives had their own careers in the music or show business, except perhaps for Rita. He shifted back to Barcelona after his fourth divorce in 1964. In 1969, he suffered a stroke which made him partially paralyzed. He died of heart failure on 27 October 1990 at the age of 90.

AN ANALYSIS OF THE RHUMBA KING

Cugat was born on a 甲Yang Wood day in the winter month of the 子Rat. As the wood was not born in the season of spring when wood is at peak strength, his wood can be considered weak at first sight. However, water nourished wood and the wood is in the growth stage during the winter season. There is also strong water available in his 亥Pig year of birth. His wood has roots in the 辰 Dragon hour of birth. Therefore, his wood is not that weak after all.

Xavier Cugat 1-1-1900

时Hour			日Day			月Month	年Year	
戊 Yang Earth			甲 Yang Wood			丙 Yang Fire	己 Yin Earth	
辰 Dragon			戌 Dog			子 Rat	亥 Pig	
戊 Yang Earth	乙 Yin Wood	癸 Yin Water	戊 Yang Earth	辛 Yin Metal	丁 Yin Fire	癸 Yin Water	壬 Yang Water	甲 Yang Wood

The strongest element in his chart was water. This water would be important to his eventual success. The strong water indicated that he was a creative and artistic person. But it was not enough to be creative. He also needed the fame star so that his artistic works could be recognized by the public. His fame star was 庚Yang Metal. He did not have this fame star in his birth chart.

Since his wood was born on a cold winter's day, he needed the fire to bring warmth to his chart. Which type of fire did he require—丙 Yang Fire or 丁Yin Fire? He needed both types of fire. The 丙Yang Fire represented the fire of the sun which provided sunlight to his 甲Yang Wood day master and brighten up his winter's day. As he was a 甲Yang Wood day master, he needed the 丁Yin Fire to burn his wood. This 丁Yin Fire represented his output or his productivity so that the fruits of his labour could be realized. In addition, he also needed the hard 庚Yang Metal that could chop down his tree to make it useful.

He was born in the 子Rat month which represented the winter season. In theory, his wood was said to be in the growth stage during winter. But the most important element that he needed, which was fire, was very weak. He also needed the庚Yang Metal.

Xavier Cugat Luck Cycle

38	28	18	8
壬 Yang Water	癸 Yin Water	甲 Yang Wood	乙 Yin Wood
申 Monkey	酉 Rooster	戌 Dog	亥 Pig
庚　壬　戊 Yang　Yang　Yang Metal　Water　Earth	辛 Yin Metal	戊　辛　丁 Yang　Yin　Yin Earth　Metal　Fire	壬　甲 Yang　Yang Water　Wood

78	68	58	48
戊 Yang Earth	己 Yin Earth	庚 Yang Metal	辛 Yin Metal
辰 Dragon	巳 Snake	午 Horse	未 Goat
戊　乙　癸 Yang　Yin　Yin Earth　Wood　Water	丙　戊　庚 Yang　Yang　Yang Fire　Earth　Metal	丁　己 Yin　Yin Fire　Earth	己　丁　乙 Yin　Yin　Yin Earth　Fire　Wood

From the age 18 until 47, he went through the luck cycles of 戌Dog, 酉Rooster and 申Monkey. These three animals represented the autumn season when metal was at peak strength. As Cugat needed metal, especially 庚Yang Metal, he was in his favourable luck period. Since his luck arrived early in his life, he found that he could achieve material success in his early youth. The庚Yang Metal arrived from the age of 38 until 47 when he commenced his 申Monkey luck cycle. This would be the best period in his life.

MANY WIVES BUT NEITHER CHILDREN NOR WEALTH

This period of autumn luck cycles was followed by the luck cycles of 未Goat, 午Horse and 巳Snake from the ages of 48 until 77. These animals represented the summer season which brought in the fire to warm his chart.

His money and his women were represented by the earth element. In the summer season, fire is strong. Fire produced earth so when fire is strong, earth is also strong. During the summer luck cycles, he had the opportunity to meet women. He married another three women from the age of 47 when he was about to commence his summer luck cycles.

However, he already had too much earth in his birth chart. There was巳Yin Earth in the Heavenly Stems above his 亥Pig year and 戊Yang Earth above his辰Dragon hour. There was also 戊Yang Earth inside his 戌Dog day and辰Dragon hour. Earth represented his money and his women. When the wealth element is too plentiful, the person would not become wealthy. Instead, he would remain poor or have to struggle with money problems all his life. He was also a womaniser and would have multiple marriages or affairs.

As this was the chart of a male, the children can only be borne by the female or his wives and mistresses. The wife star was represented by the earth element which in turn produced the metal element. Therefore, his children were represented by metal.

He was born in the winter season. Metal is weak during winter. The strongest element in winter was water. There was also water available in his 亥Pig year. But too much water would cause the metal to sink in the water. The only metal available in his chart was in his 戌Dog day of birth. So the weak metal was buried by the excessive earth and further weakened by the strong water. He would have difficulty in making his wives pregnant. His wives also might have some difficulty conceiving children. But if the central problem lay with him, then no matter how many wives he married would not have made much difference.

In 1948, he published his autobiography, *"Rhumba is My Life."* With the passage of time, this book is no longer in print. Depending

5

on how candid he was or was not in his autobiography, his book might or might not have helped to clarify certain issues.

For instance, did any of his wives have other husbands before or after their marriages to him? If so, did his wives bear any children to their other husbands? If his wives could give birth to children after marrying other husbands, then it would show that his wives were not infertile women.

SHOW ME THE MONEY, MASTER!

There were media reports that he owned as many as eight restaurants. This would have made him appear wealthy on paper. But he was a performing musician and was busy with performances and recordings. How could he ever spare the time attending to the restaurant business, which was a full time occupation?

If he ventured into the restaurant business, he had to do so with other partners. In that case, he would have to share whatever profits derived from the restaurants with his partners. There might not have been very much of the profits left over for a dormant partner. As he had multiple divorces, he was required to pay a fair amount of alimony. If he had kept up his alimony payments, they would have been a drain on his finances.

The only significance of the restaurants was that their interiors were decorated with his art work. But Xavier Cugat was remembered as a musician and band leader, not as an artist or even an entrepreneur in the restaurant business. If not for his music, he would have been forgotten today.

He was not known for his compositions but for his performances. His band played or popularised the music composed by such eminent names as Ernesto Lecuona *("Siboney"),* Sebastian Yradier *("La Paloma"),* Alberto Dominguez *("Perfidia")* or Aro Barroso *("Brazil")* and traditional tunes such as *"La Cucaracha"* ("The Cockroach") or *"Jarabe Tapatio"* ("Mexican Hat Dance").

WHERE WERE THE CHILDREN?

His women were represented by earth. Since earth produced metal, his children were represented by metal. He was born in the 子Rat month which represented the winter season. Both the earth and metal elements were weak during winter. In winter, water was the strongest element. The earth element required fire to produce it. The metal element was strongest during the autumn season.

This structure indicated that he may have many wives but his wives would have difficulty conceiving, despite their youth and beauty.

The metal was the weakest element in his birth chart. The only metal present was the 辛Yin Metal in his 戌Dog day of birth. The overly strong water weakened the metal and made it sink in the pool of water.

He was born in the 辰Dragon hour. The hour pillar represented children. This辰Dragon hour clashed with his 戌Dog day master. This meant that his weak metal in the戌Dog was clashed away by the辰Dragon. His children star was already clashed out. He would not be close to his children, even if had adopted any children.

DO CHILDREN MATTER?

So what if he did not have any children? Were children important in a marriage? The answer would depend on the background and culture of the reader. In most cultures, it was usually implied that the purpose of the marriage was to produce children. If the marriage was childless, it would be regarded as a failure of sorts on the part of the couple. Human society required children to continue the human species. In time, children would grow up and look after their parents in their old age. In Chinese culture, one of the reasons for desiring children is the hope that they can bury and pray for their ancestors upon their deaths.

In practical terms, if the parents were wealthy, they could leave behind their estates to their children. If there were no children, most governments would take away the estate in the form of taxes. Since

Chapter One

Cugat was a musician, he could have left behind royalties from his recordings. However, this was a moot question as he died childless despite having many wives. In his old age, he had no children to look after him. It was a sad ending for the maestro of rhumba.

CHAPTER TWO

"TWO WOMEN"

"God bless you, please, Mrs Robinson,
Heaven holds a place for those who pray,
Hey, hey, hey . . . Hey, hey, hey . . . "
(Simon and Garfunkel song, *"Mrs Robinson"* from *"The Graduate"*, 1968)

"THEIR TURNING POINT"

Anne Bancroft and Shirley MacLaine made only one movie together in their lengthy careers. In 1970, they danced their way in *"The Turning Point."* Both of them were trained dancers so they had no difficulty in dancing opposite their leading man, Mikhail Baryshnikov. After their spectacular dancing effort, they never collaborated any more.

In that case, why write about them? Why mention them in the same breath? There are several reasons why they can be considered together in an article. Both of them shared the same day master. They were both born on a 乙 Yin Wood day. But there the similarity ended. Bancroft was a weak wood person, MacLaine was a strong wood person. Both had distinguished careers but Bancroft made fewer movies and was more selective in her choice of roles. Bancroft was more reserved, MacLaine was more outspoken. And so the list goes on. The similarities and the differences probably make for a compelling tale.

The original *"Two Women" ("La Ciociara")* was a novel written in 1946 by the Italian novelist, Alberto Moravia. The first English translation was made in 1957. The Penguin translation by Angus Davidson was published in 1961. It was made into a movie starring Sophia Loren. This movie would launch Sophia Loren into stardom and win her an Oscar. The story concerned a widow and her teenage daughter caught in the throes of the Second World War when the Anglo-American armies invade southern Italy.

Sophia Loren was a budding star who was often compared to her rival, Gina Lollobrigida. In that sense, it could be said these were the original "two women." We have borrowed the term from Alberto Moravia and applied it to another "two women" whose lives were just as interesting as the Italian two women.

To begin with, both Anne Bancroft and Shirley MacLaine had been trained as dancers. Both of them acted mostly in non-dancing roles throughout their careers. Why did they train as dancers but accepted mostly non-dancing roles? MacLaine explained that she was only an average dancer and could not perform the more difficult dance moves very well. Bancroft trained from age four and MacLaine from age five.

Then both of them were born on the same wood day. Bancroft and MacLaine were born on a 乙 Yin Wood day. But there the similarity ended. Their day master was different. Bancroft was born on a 亥 Pig day whereas MacLaine was born on a 丑 Ox day. The differences outweigh the similarities. Yet each of them achieved success in their respective acting careers. That was reason enough for us to tell their story together.

THE WEAK WOOD PERSON—ANNE BANCROFT

Anne Bancroft was born as Anna Maria Louisa Italiano in The Bronx to Italian parents, Michael Italiano and Mildred DiNapoli. She appeared in TV dramas as Anne Marno and changed her stage name when she made her film debut in *"Don't Bother to Knock"*, released in 1952.

Anne Bancroft will probably be forever remembered as Mrs. Robinson in *"The Graduate"*.

Anne Bancroft was born on a 乙 Yin Wood day in the 酉 Rooster month. This month represented the autumn season when metal was at peak strength. Since metal is the antithesis of wood, when metal is strong, it stands to reason that wood must be weak. Therefore, Bancroft's wood is considered weak because her wood was not born in season. However, her wood has roots in her 亥 Pig day and 未 Goat year.

Anne Bancroft 17-9-1931

时 Hour	日 Day	月 Month	年 Year
壬 Yang Water	乙 Yin Wood	丁 Yin Fire	辛 Yin Metal
午 Horse	亥 Pig	酉 Rooster	未 Goat
丁　　已 Yin　　Yin Fire　　Earth	壬　　甲 Yang　　Yang Water　　Wood	辛 Yin Metal	已　　丁　　乙 Yin　　Yin　　Yin Earth　　Fire　　Wood

She needs 癸Yin Water which represented rain water to nourish her wood and make it grow. As she was born in the cool autumn season, she also needed fire to warm her chart. She already had the 丁Yin Fire in her chart. She only needed the 丙Yang Fire which represented the fire of the sun. When she encountered the癸Yin Water and the丙Yang Fire in her luck cycles, then her luck would improve.

Anne Bancroft Luck Cycle

37	27	17	7
辛 Yin Metal	庚 Yang Metal	己 Yin Earth	戊 Yang Earth
丑 Ox	子 Rat	亥 Pig	戌 Dog
己 癸 辛 Yin Yin Yin Earth Water Metal	癸 Yin Water	壬 甲 Yang Yang Water Wood	戊 辛 丁 Yang Yin Yin Earth Metal Fire

77	67	57	47
乙 Yin Wood	甲 Yang Wood	癸 Yin Water	壬 Yang Water
巳 Snake	辰 Dragon	卯 Rabbit	寅 Tiger
丙 戊 庚 Yang Yang Yang Fire Earth Metal	戊 乙 癸 Yang Yin Yin Earth Wood Water	乙 Yin Wood	甲 丙 戊 Yang Yang Yang Wood Fire Earth

Her 子Rat luck cycle from the age of 27 brought the癸Yin Water that she needed. Then her 寅Tiger luck cycle from the age of 47 introduced the丙Yang Fire into her life. That explained why she won her first Tony award in 1958 when she turned 27. She won another Tony award in 1960 and her Oscar in 1963. In 1964 she won acclaim for her appearance in *"The Pumpkin Eater"*. This was the year of 甲Yang Wood 辰Dragon when the wood is strong in the spring season. Bancroft needed this support as her wood day master was weak.

If she achieved some success with *"The Pumpkin Eater"*, there would be even more accolades for her in the near future. It was her role as Mrs Robinson in *"The Graduate"* in 1967 for which she would probably forever be remembered. This movie helped to launch the career of Dustin Hoffman and was memorable for the music of Paul Simon and Art Garfunkel. The year 1967 was the year of 丁Yin Fire 未Goat. As the 未Goat represented the summer season, it brought the much needed丁Yin Fire into the life of Bancroft.

In 1977, she capped her success by acting in *"The Turning Point."* The year 1977 was the year of 丁Yin Fire 巳Snake. In that year, she had both the 丁Yin Fire and the 丙Yang Fire that she needed. There was 丁Yin Fire in the year's Heavenly Stem and there was丙Yang Fire inside the巳Snake year. This was a good year for her. The丙Yang Fire represented the fire of the sun which was needed to grow her wood. The巳Snake year clashed with her 亥Pig day of birth. This was a good clash. Not all clashes in astrology are bad clashes.

Bancroft married Martin May in July 1953 and divorced in February 1957. They had no children from this marriage. The year 1953 was the year of 癸Yin Water 巳Snake. The 巳Snake year contained metal which represented her boyfriend or husband star. The year 1957 was the year of 丁Yin Fire 酉Rooster. She was aged 26 when she divorced. This meant that she was in her酉Rooster month of birth during that age period. The丁Yin Fire 酉Rooster year had a self-punishment relationship with her month of birth. The self-punishment affected the metal inside the 酉Rooster year and her丁Yin Fire 酉Rooster month of birth. This indicated that her marriage was under stress. However, it did not mean that divorce was inevitable.

Her second marriage was happier and lasted until her death in June 2005. She married fellow actor Mel Brooks and had a son,

Maximillian Brooks in 1972. She was a more reserved person than MacLaine. She valued her privacy so much that it was not publicly known that she suffered from uterine cancer until after her death.

THE STRONG WOOD PERSON—SHIRLEY MACLAINE

Shirley MacLaine was born as Shirley MacLean Beaty in Richmond to Ira Owens Beaty and Kathlyn Corrine. Her father was a psychology professor and her mother taught drama. Her brother was Warren Beaty who became a successful actor. She attended ballet classes as a child, perhaps as early as two years old. However, she did not eventually pursue a career as a dancer. Among the reasons she cited were that she was too tall and did not have a dancer's feet to give her the flair of a professional dancer.

In 1954, she was the understudy to Carol Haney in *"The Pyjama Game"*. When Haney broke her ankle, MacLaine replaced her. During one performance, the producer Hal Wallis was in the audience. He was impressed enough to sign her to his studio, Paramount Pictures.

Shirley MacLaine was also born on a 乙 Yin Wood day. But she was born in the 辰 Dragon month which represented the spring season. So that means her wood is strong because the wood was born in season. There was also 甲 Yang Wood in the Heavenly Stems above her 戌 Dog year and 甲 Monkey hour.

Shirley MacLaine 24-4-1934

时Hour	日Day	月Month	年Year
甲 Yang Wood	乙 Yin Wood	戊 Yang Earth	甲 Yang Wood
申 Monkey	丑 Ox	辰 Dragon	戌 Dog
庚　壬　戊 Yang Yang Yang Metal Water Earth	己　癸　辛 Yin Yin Yin Earth Water Metal	戊　乙　癸 Yang Yin Yin Earth Wood Water	戊　辛　丁 Yang Yin Yin Earth Metal Fire

This 甲 Yang Wood would be important to her 乙 Yin Wood. The 乙 Yin Wood represented small plants such as creepers and vines. These types of plants needed the tall trees represented by 甲 Yang Wood to cling and climb upwards to reach the sunlight. She needed 癸 Yin Water which represented rain water and 丙 Yang Fire which represented sunlight to grow her wood.

But this structure also made the wood too strong. When the wood was overly strong, the person would be too drawn to spiritual or religious matters. This would also make the person outspoken and aggressive. She would certainly speak her mind. These traits were evidenced by the nine books that she wrote from 1982. All of her books were biographical in nature with large doses of New Age spirituality, reincarnation and even UFO sightings. Although her books were autobiographical, they were not useful to the researcher because they dwelled too much on spiritual matters than on biographical facts. For instance, in one of her books, she believed that she had been reincarnated before the age of seven.

In 1954, she married producer Steve Parker. When he returned to Japan, MacLaine had to stay in California due to her work commitments. In 1955, their only child, Stephanie Sachiko, better known as Sachi Parker, was born. When their daughter was about seven years old, she went to Japan to stay with her father. The couple separated some time in the mid-1970s and divorced by 1983. Later, MacLaine publicly admitted that she had several affairs during her marriage.

WAS WEAK WOOD OR STRONG WOOD BETTER?

Both women had successful careers as actress. Each of them won numerous awards throughout their lengthy careers. Despite their early training as dancers, neither of them appeared in movies or the theatre that required dancing. The only notable exception was their joint appearance in *"The Turning Point"* in 1977.

But the criteria for assessing whether or not a female life was successful did not depend on the career. In traditional times, the assessment was based on whether the female had a happy marriage and raised a family. Even in the modern twenty first century, astrologers who practice the ancient art of Chinese astrology still use this method to determine whether the female lived a fulfilled life. If the female had a successful career but did not marry or married but did not have any children, we still claim that such a person had not fulfilled her destiny.

Who had the happier marriage? Bancroft married twice. The first marriage was short lived and ended in divorce without any children. The second marriage lasted until her death more than 40 years later. She had one son from the second marriage.

Shirley MacLaine Luck Cycle

36	26		16	6
甲 Yang Wood	乙 Yin Wood		丙 Yang Fire	丁 Yin Fire
子 Rat	丑 Ox		寅 Tiger	卯 Rabbit
癸 Yin Water	己 Yin Earth	癸 辛 Yin Yin Water Metal	甲 丙 戊 Yang Yang Yang Wood Fire Earth	乙 Yin Wood

76	66	56	46
庚 Yang Metal	辛 Yin Metal	壬 Yang Water	癸 Yin Water
申 Monkey	酉 Rooster	戌 Dog	亥 Pig
庚 壬 戊 Yang Yang Yang Metal Water Earth	辛 Yin Metal	戊 辛 丁 Yang Yin Yin Earth Metal Fire	壬 甲 Yang Yang Water Wood

Shirley MacLaine married only once. Her marriage was also long lasting, almost 30 years from 1954 until 1982. She also had only one child from her marriage. But although her marriage lasted a long time, she confessed that there were affairs during the marriage. So the marriage could not have been such a happy union after all despite the long duration of the marriage.

How do we know that Bancroft had the happier marriage? To a wood female, the husband star is represented by metal. There was metal in her 酉 Rooster month of birth. The month of birth can be said to represent the marriage pillar because most people get married during their twenties or thirties. The month pillar was also said to be located close to the day master. Her 酉 Rooster month of birth did not clash with her 亥 Pig day of birth.

Conversely, why did we argue that MacLaine had an unhappier union despite her lengthy marriage? As she was also a wood female, her husband star was likewise represented by metal. The wood is very strong in her chart because she was born in the spring season. When wood was strong, metal had to be weak since metal was the antithesis of wood. There was metal in her 戌 Dog year, 丑 Ox day and 申 Monkey hour. Although the metal was weak, there was too much metal in her chart. This indicated that the person would probably have affairs with several men even if these affairs did not result in marriage.

Who was closer to her only child? To a female wood person, the children star was represented by fire. The fire was weak in Bancroft's chart because she was born in autumn. However, there was fire in her 午 Horse hour of birth. The hour of birth also represented the children's palace. Her 午 Horse hour did not clash with her 亥 Pig day of birth. This indicated that she was close to her son.

The only fire in MacLaine's chart was located in her 戌 Dog year of birth. It was the hour of birth that represented the children's pillar, not the year of birth which represented her childhood. The absence of fire in the hour of birth showed that she could not have been close to her only child. There were also other indications in her chart. The fire was weak in her chart since she was born in the spring season. Her 申 Monkey hour of birth only had a neutral relationship instead of a harmonious relationship with her 丑 Ox day of birth.

As the wood was overly strong in MacLaine's chart, the person would be too drawn to spiritual matters. She would be so fixed in her views that she could not accept the opinions of other people. This characteristic would make the person narrow in her thinking and outlook. Her books might have sold well but it probably appealed more to readers who were more interested in spiritual, out of body matters rather than for whatever biographical detail revealed in the books.

Perhaps it could also be pointed out that for all the numerous appearances in film and on stage, there was no defining role or character that could be identified with Shirley MacLaine. In the case of Anne Bancroft, she would probably be forever remembered as Mrs Robinson in *"The Graduate."*

So it does not mean that being a strong day master is preferable to being a weak day master. One must analyse the overall structure of the chart to make a meaningful assessment. Both weak and strong day master persons may have potential for achievement. How much is that potential and when the achievement will come will depend on the luck cycles.

CHAPTER THREE

HE HAD WOOD IN HIS CHART. SO WHY WASN'T ADOLF HITLER KIND?

*"I go the way that Providence dictates with
the assurance of a sleepwalker . . ."*
(Hitler, speech at Munich, March 1936)

In the study of Chinese astrology, the element wood is often associated with kindness and benevolence. Adolf Hitler was born on 20 April 1889. This meant that he was born in the spring season. Wood is at peak strength in the spring season. Hitler not only had wood in his birth chart; his wood was also very strong.

Yet Hitler is remembered in history not for his benevolence but for the Holocaust which exterminated some six million Jews. Surely such an act cannot be considered kind by any standards.

Why did a person who had such strong wood commit atrocities? Were there some flaws in the traditional astrology theories? Or could there be some other explanation for the exception to the rule?

In December 1923, Hitler was arrested and jailed for his part in a failed coup. By January 1933, he had been appointed Chancellor of Germany. What brought about the change in his flagging fortunes within a mere decade?

PART I: THE HISTORY

THE EARLY YEARS OF REJECTION AND FAILURE

Adolf Hitler was born on 20 April 1889 in Braunau, Austria to Alois Hitler and Klara Poelzl. His father was a local customs official. He was the fourth of six children, three of whom died in infancy during a diphtheria outbreak in 1887-1888. In June 1895, his father retired and tried unsuccessfully to become a farmer. His father was strict with him which resulted in conflict between them. He sang in the school choir and initially wanted to become a priest. After his brother Edmund died from measles on 2 February 1900 at the age of 16, he became sullen and morose.

His father died on 3 January 1903. In 1905, he left school at the age of 16 without obtaining any formal qualifications. One of his fellow pupils at his Realschule was the future philosopher, Ludwig Wittgenstein. In 1907, he applied at the Academy of Fine Arts, Vienna to study painting. The Academy rejected him then and again in 1908 due to his "lack of ability." Instead, he was advised to study architecture.

His mother died on 21 December 1907. A Jewish doctor attended to her. He did not seem to harbour any grudges against the Jews for his mother's death. He was saddened by the death of his mother more than the death of his father. His father did not allow him to claim any inheritance until he reached the age of 24. In the meantime, he lived on the inheritance from his mother.

He did not seek any employment after his parents' death. Instead, he chose to eke out a living by making postcard drawings of buildings in Vienna. His drawings usually did not feature any human beings, only buildings. By 1909, his money ran out and he lived in a shelter for the homeless. At that time, there was a strong feeling of religious prejudice and racism in Vienna. But Hitler did not seem to have any racial prejudices against the Jews at this period.

"THE WAR THAT MADE HITLER POSSIBLE"

In 1913, he went to Munich to avoid being drafted into the Austrian army. In February 1914, he failed his physical examination and was rejected by the Austrian army. When war broke out in August 1914, he tried to join the Bavarian army. He was rejected by the Bavarian King's Own Regiment but was accepted by Bavarian Reserve Infantry Regiment 16 (List Regiment).

Hitler was a despatch runner at the regimental level. The regimental headquarters was usually based far behind the Front, unlike the battalion or company runners. Hitler was not in the line of fire. But he came into contact with senior officers in the regiment who recommended him for the Iron Cross.

In 1917, he was awarded the Iron Cross, Second Class for bravery. In August the same year, he was given the Iron Cross, First Class. In May 1918, he was also awarded the Black Wound Badge. The Iron Cross was rarely awarded to soldiers of such low rank. Hitler never rose above the rank of corporal. The regiment's adjutant, Hugo Guttman, was a Jew who helped to recommend him for the medal. For his pains, he would later be imprisoned by the Gestapo.

There was some discussion of promoting Hitler to a non-commissioned officer but nothing came of it because they "could discover no leadership qualities in him."

Hitler was wounded at the Somme in October 1916 in the groin or the left thigh. In October 1918, he was blinded by a gas mustard attack near Comines, Ypres. He was sent to a hospital at Pasewalk,

Pomerania. While he was still at the hospital, the Armistice was signed in November 1918. He also heard that Kaiser Wilhelm II had abdicated and went into exile in the Netherlands. Germany became the Weimar Republic.

Hitler blamed the woes of Germany on *die Dolchstosslegende* ("the stab in the back"). The German army which was undefeated in the battlefield had been betrayed by the "November criminals" who in turn were said to be influenced by the Jews.

POLITICS AND PRISON

When he left the army in March 1920, he had no money and no prospects of getting any. He had squandered the inheritance he was given by his deceased parents. The definitive biography of Hitler was written by Ian Kershaw in his encyclopaedic two volumes, *"Hitler, 1889-1936: Hubris"* (Penguin, 1998) and *"Hitler, 1936-1945: Nemesis"* (Penguin, 2000). He summed it succinctly when he wrote that the First World War was "the war that made Hitler possible."

Hitler was given the task to influence other soldiers and infiltrate the German Workers Party (DAP). He met Anton Drexler who influenced him with anti-Semitic, anti-Marxist and anti-capitalist ideas. He became the 55th member of the DAP. The name of the party was changed to German National Socialist Workers Party (NSDAP) or Nazi Party.

He began a series of rowdy, polemic beer hall speeches. In June 1921, some members of the NSDAP wanted to merge with the weak German Socialist Party (DSP). Hitler threatened to resign from the party. The party realised that if he resigned, the party would have lost its public face. So when he demanded that he replaced Drexler as chairman as the condition for remaining with the party, they agreed.

On 8-9 November 1923, Hitler staged a putsch to try and seize power in Munich. He had the support of General Erich Ludendorff. He planned to organise a march to Berlin. He was inspired by Mussolini's march to Rome in October 1922. But the putsch failed when the Bavarian government sent the police to supress the coup.

Sixteen people were killed. While Ludendorff was acquitted in the ensuing trial, Hitler was not. He was jailed for five years but served only nine months in Landsberg prison.

His term in prison was not penitential. Winifred Wagner, the British daughter-in-law of Richard Wagner (whose operas Hitler admired) sent him food and stationery. She urged him to write his memoirs. He was too idle to write anything. Instead, he dictated his memoirs to Rudolf Hess and Emil Maurice. The memoirs were later published as *"Mein Kampf"* ("My Struggle").

THE LEGAL ROAD TO POWER

The Treaty of Versailles stipulated that Germany had to pay reparations for war damages inflicted on France during the war. But the amount of reparations was not specified. Instead, the amount was open ended and left to be decided later. These terms implied that when the German economy recovered, the payments would be increased. There was no incentive for the Germans to rebuild their economy.

On 11 January 1923, French troops occupied the Rhineland which produced eighty per cent of the steel, iron and coal of Germany. Without the resources of the Rhineland, the Germans could not pay the reparations. The Rhineland was declared a demilitarised zone.

The provisions of the Treaty caused resentment to linger among the Germans. When Hitler sought to renege the terms of the Treaty, he had the widespread support of the German population. The statesmen who drafted the Treaty in 1918 had unwittingly played into Hitler's hands.

The crippling effects of the Versailles Treaty on the German economy were exacerbated when the American stock market crashed on 24 October 1929.

The Great Depression that followed caused runaway inflation and widespread unemployment to about 5 million workers in Germany. The German government fell in March 1930. Heinrich

Bruning, the leader of the Catholic Centre Right Party, was appointed Chancellor. He dissolved the *Reichstag* or Parliament.

In May 1928 the Nazi party won only a mere 2.6 per cent of the vote which gave them 12 seats in the *Reichstag*. In the next elections, the Nazi Party won 107 seats which made it the largest party with one fifth of the Reichstag seats. Bruning offered Hitler to form a coalition government which he refused.

On 18 September 1931, Hitler's niece Geli Rabual committed suicide. She was the daughter of his half-sister, Angela Rabual. Geli became his housekeeper and female companion from 1925. Hitler was devastated and depressed for two days, refusing to attend her funeral.

In the July 1932 elections, the Nazi party won 37.4 per cent of the vote. It was unprecedented that a major European state had voted against democracy.

The President, Paul von Hindenburg, appointed Franz von Papen Chancellor. In August 1932, Papen offered Hitler the post of Vice Chancellor. President Hindenburg had a close adviser, the right wing Kurt von Schleicher who offered the post of Chancellor to Georg Strasser. But Strasser did not have the backing of the Nazi party. By January 1933, Papen advised President Hindenburg to appoint Hitler Chancellor but on the condition that only two seats in the Cabinet were occupied by Nazis and the rest by Conservatives. Papen also wanted to oust Schleicher as Chancellor.

After Hitler became Chancellor, he dissolved the Reichstag for fresh elections that would grant him emergency powers. His SA and Stahlhelm units marched in a procession in Berlin. Ludendorff prophesied to Hindenburg that Hitler would bring ruin to Germany. He also warned him that future generations would condemn Hindenburg for appointing Hitler as Chancellor.

On 2 August 1934, President Hindenburg died. In addition to being Chancellor, Hitler also replaced Hindenburg as the President. On 19 August, he held a plebiscite that he should be called Furher or the Leader instead of both Chancellor and President. The result was that 89.9 per cent of the Germans voted in favour of the proposal. Hitler came to power the legal way, he did not seize power.

The Germans supported Hitler because his government managed to solve the unemployment crisis and bring about an economic recovery. The Minister of Economics, Hjalmar Schacht, had achieved full employment by implementing public works schemes, building motor highways and mass employment in the armaments factories to build aircraft and tanks.

THE DARK SIDE BEGINS—THE NIGHT OF THE LONG KNIVES

On 27 February 1933, a Dutchman, Marinus van der Lubbe set fire to the Reichstag or parliament building. Hindenburg was persuaded to suspend civil liberties. This resulted in the detention of thousands of people in concentration camps. The persecution of the Jews had already begun even before the outbreak of the Second World War in September 1939. On 30 June 1934, he ordered the start of the "Night of the Long Knives" or the Rohm Putsch when Ernest Rohm and other SA *("Sturmabteilung")* were murdered.

However, Hitler was not the only dictator to eliminate his rivals. In ancient history, there have been many Emperors and Sultans who disposed of their rivals to the throne. In modern history, his contemporary Josef Stalin probably killed even more people than Hitler when he implemented his Great Purge from 1936 to 1938.

THE BLUNDERS THAT LED TO WAR—(1) AUSTRIA AND THE *ANSCHLUSS*

On 25 July 1934, the Austrian Chancellor, Engelbert Dollfuss was murdered by the Austrian Nazis who tried to seize power in Vienna. His successor, Kurt von Schuschnigg put down the rebellion with the help of Italian troops sent by Mussolini.

In a referendum in March 1936, Austrians overwhelmingly voted for *Anschluss* or political union with Germany. This was in violation of the Treaty of Versailles. The Treaty did not take into account the views of the Austrians who had already voted in 1918 for reunification.

In February 1938, Schuschnigg tried to placate Hitler by appointing Arthur Sessy-Inquart as Minister of the Interior. Sessy-Inquart was an active member of the Fascist Party in Austria. Once Hitler was assured that Mussolini would not intervene, his troops marched into Austria on 12 March 1938. Schuschnigg was arrested and replaced by Sessy-Inquart as Chancellor.

The historian AJP Taylor argued in *"The Origins of the Second World War"* (Penguin, 1961) that so far what Hitler had done was perfectly legal. After all, the Austrians had taken a vote and they had chosen to unite with Germany. AJP Taylor went on to argue that Hitler or Germany did not cause the Second World War. Instead, Hitler blundered into war, aided and abetted by the blunders of the statesmen of that era—especially the British and the French. At that time, such views were controversial and upset the leading historians of the day, such as Alan Bullock and Hugh Trevor-Roper, who blamed Hitler for starting the next war.

But Hitler also had many non-German admirers. In December 1933, Lord Rothermere, the owner of the British newspaper, the *Daily Mail* and his editor, Ward Price dined with Hitler. The *Daily Mail* would write reports in support of Hitler and Germany for several years afterwards. The British Liberal Party leader, Lloyd George also openly admired Hitler when he visited Germany. In Germany, even intellectuals such as the philosopher Martin Heidegger admired Hitler.

THE BLUNDERS THAT LED TO WAR—(2) CZECHSOLOVAKIA AND THE SUDETENLAND

The Sudetenland was the north west region of Czechoslovakia which had a sizeable German population. This gave rise to political tensions between the Czechs and the Germans. The Paris Peace Conference of 1919 allotted the Sudetenland to Czechoslovakia.

In May 1935, the Sudeten-German Party (SdP) in Czechoslovakia won 63 % of the votes. Konrad Henlein, the leader of the SdP, began to make exaggerated demands on the Czech government which were impossible to meet. This gave Hitler the excuse to make an attempt to annex the Sudetenland.

The President, Edvard Benes, hoped that the British and the French would provide military intervention. On 15 September 1938, the British Prime Minister Neville Chamberlain met Hitler in Munich for discussions. The Czechs were excluded from the discussions. On 19 September, Chamberlain and the French Prime Minister Edouard Daladier presented Benes with a *fait accompli*—they told Benes to cede the Sudetenland to Hitler.

On 29 September 1938, Neville Chamberlain signed the Munich Agreement with Hitler in the presence of Daladier and Benito Mussolini. Hitler was allowed to annex the Sudetenland but not to occupy the rest of Czechoslovakia. This Agreement did not deter German troops from marching into Prague on 15 March 1939.

THE DARK SIDE CONTINUED—THE *KRISTALLNACHT* (THE NIGHT OF BROKEN GLASS)

On 9 November 1938, a Polish Jew, Herschel Grynszpan, went to the German Embassy in Paris and shot the first diplomat he saw. The victim was a minor official, Ernst von Rath. This incident was known as *Kristallnacht* (the Night of the Broken Glass). It provoked Joseph Goebbels, the Propaganda Minister, to launch a pogrom against the Jews. Some 7,500 Jewish shops and most synagogues were destroyed throughout Germany. From 9 to 16 November, an estimated 30,000 Jews were sent to concentration camps in Dachau, Buchenwald and Sachsenhausen.

THE BLUNDERS THAT LED TO WAR—(3) POLAND AND THE DANZIG CORRIDOR

After the war, Poland had expanded her borders to such an extent that it created tensions with all her neighbours except Romania. There were border disputes over Teschen with Czechoslovakia and over Vilnius with Lithuania. The Treaty of Versailles granted the

Danzig Corridor to give land locked Poland access to a neutral port. The Germans were resentful over the loss of the Danzig Corridor.

Hitler annexed the Danzig Corridor and invaded Poland on 1 September 1939. Britain and France had a treaty with Poland. They declared war with Germany on 3 September 1939. Hitler was surprised that "the little worms" as he called Daladier and Chamberlain would go to war over Poland.

EARLY VICTORIES AND EVENTUAL DEFEAT

On 17 September 1939, the Soviet Union attacked Poland from the east. Poland capitulated on 27 September. The German armies invaded Norway on 9 April 1940 followed by the Low Countries and France on 10 May 1940. By late May, General Gerd von Rundstedt stopped the advance of the German tanks near Dunkirk to wait for the slower infantry to catch up. The chief of the army, General Walter von Brauchitsch and his chief of staff, General Franz Halder were so furious with this order that they transferred back command of the Panzers to Army Group B.

Hitler overruled their decision and agreed with Rundstedt that there should be a halt. He had intervened to show that the imminent victory in France was due to him rather than to his generals. This famous halt order allowed the bulk of the British Expeditionary Force (BEF) to be evacuated from 26 May to 4 June 1940. The war that could have been won for him by his generals was lost by him because he wanted to show his generals who was in charge.

The next mistake Hitler made was to order the *Luftwaffe* to bomb British cities instead of airfields as a reprisal for the RAF's bombing of Berlin. He broke the Hitler-Stalin Pact of 1939 by launching *Operation Barbarossa* on 22 June 1941 to invade the Soviet Union. On 11 December 1941, after the Japanese attacked Pearl Harbour, Hitler foolishly declared war on the United States. By fighting two powers that had vast manpower and industrial resources, Hitler had already lost the war for Germany.

THE DARK SIDE EXPANDED—"THE FINAL SOLUTION"

It was the invasion of Russia that gave Hitler the opportunity to implement "The Final Solution". In July 1941, he ordered the construction of concentration camps for the Jews. As Poland had the greatest numbers of Jews, most of these camps were located in Poland.

On 20 January 1942, Hitler held the Wannsee Conference of top Nazi officials and sanctioned the *Endlosung* ("The Final Solution") or the mass extermination of the Jews.

Hitler had misapplied the concept of the *Ubermencsh* ("the Superman") espoused by the philosopher Friedrich Nietzsche to mean the superiority of the Aryan race over other races such as the Jews.

PART II: THE ASTROLOGY

THE EARLY YEARS ANALYSED

Hitler was born on a 丙Yang Fire day in the 辰Dragon month. The 辰Dragon month represented the spring season when wood was the strongest element. His fire day master is considered fairly strong because fire was in the growth stage in spring. His fire was also rooted in his 寅Tiger day of birth.

Adolf Hitler 20-4-1889

时Hour	日Day			月Month			年Year		
丁 Yin Fire	丙 Yang Fire			戊 Yang Earth			己 Yin Earth		
酉 Rooster	寅 Tiger			辰 Dragon			丑 Ox		
辛 Yin Metal	甲 Yang Wood	丙 Yang Fire	戊 Yang Earth	戊 Yang Earth	乙 Yin Wood	癸 Yin Water	己 Yin Earth	癸 Yin Water	辛 Yin Metal

As his fire was fairly strong, the elements that he needed in his life were 壬 Yang Water to cool down his chart and 甲 Yang Wood. If his wood element was already strong, why did he require even more 甲 Yang Wood? The reason was that the earth was still hard in the 辰 Dragon month and 寅 Tiger day. The 甲 Yang Wood was needed to loosen the earth so that the 壬 Yang Water could flow more easily. He only had the 甲 Yang Wood in his birth chart. This meant that when he encountered 壬 Yang Water in his luck cycles, his fortunes would improve. His 壬 Yang Water would arrive when he reached the age of 45 in 1934, one year after he became Chancellor of Germany.

Initially, he expressed interest to become a priest. Why was he attracted to the clergy? His strongest element was wood since he was born in the spring season. The wood element represented, among other things, spiritual and religious matters. Later in his life, he would become too superstitious which made him prone to deception by the Allies.

The death of his brother in 1900 changed his outlook. It probably caused him to abandon any desire to become a priest. Instead, he became sullen and withdrawn. He was then 11 years old.

Since he was born on a 丙 Yang Fire day, his fire was produced by wood. The wood element represented his mother. In turn, the wood element was controlled by the metal element which represented his father. He had a difficult relationship with his father who was strict with him. He was born on a 寅 Tiger day in the 辰 Dragon month. His wood was very strong and he could resist the conflict with his father. His father died in 1903 when he was 13 years old.

After his father died, he could choose to drop out of school. He wanted to become a painter. But the Academy of Fine Arts rejected him twice. Hitler was neither imaginative nor creative. His water element was weak in the spring season. Why was water so important to creativity? Water represented intelligence and imagination. When water was weak, the person was not likely to have the imagination so necessary for artistic creativity. Hitler only had some water in his 丑 Ox year and 辰 Dragon month. The weak water had been used up to nourish the strong wood in spring. The Academy made the right decision to reject him in 1907 (the 丁 Yin Fire 未 Goat year) and 1908 (the 戊 Yang Earth 申 Monkey year). He was then aged 18 and 19. The 未 Goat year clashed with his 丑 Ox year of birth. The 申 Monkey year clashed with his 寅 Tiger day master.

His mother died in 1907 which was the 丁 Yin Fire 未 Goat year. In the 未 Goat year, the wood element was said to be in storage or in the graveyard. This meant that the wood element was weak. The wood element represented the mother. It was possible that the mother might become sick and in severe cases, perhaps even die.

He was too idle to seek employment. He survived on his mother's inheritance. His father stipulated that he could not claim his inheritance until reached 24 years old in 1913. His wood element was his resource element because wood provided the fuel for his fire. Since fire produced earth, his output element was earth. But earth was weak in spring. The weak water already indicated that he was not bright academically nor creative in an artistic way. So he was not only stupid, he was also indolent.

In fact, he was probably too dumb to start a war on his own initiative. Professor AJP Taylor had a point when he argued that the statesmen of the day blundered into war with Hitler.

Hitler ruled by bullying and bluster, by a policy of divide and conquer. There was ample historical evidence that showed many instances when he played off one subordinate against the other. He was a bully and like most bullies, he felt insecure. He lacked the guile of a Metternich, the cunning of a Machiavelli.

There was also sufficient historical evidence to show that the German High Command did not want war or at least wanted to postpone war. Admiral Erich Raeder of the *Kreigsmarine* elicited a promise from Hitler that "there would be no war until 1943." This unwarlike situation was very different from the mood in Japan where the military was bent on seeking war but Admiral Yamamoto wanted to avoid war.

Yet one day such an idle person would become the future Chancellor of Germany. Why?

AN ANALYSIS OF HIS LEGAL ROAD TO POWER

This 壬 Yang Water arrived at the age of 45 in 1934 when he was in his 亥 Pig luck cycle. The 壬 Yang Water also represented his authority and power star. On 2 August 1934, President Paul von Hindenburg died. Hitler became both President and Chancellor. He called himself the Fuhrer (or Leader). By then, he had become Chancellor for about a year, in 1933. If his 亥 Pig luck cycle brought him his authority star, then how was it that he achieved high position one year ago?

Date Hitler appointed Chancellor 30-1-1933

时 Hour?	日 Day			月 Month			年 Year		
	丙 Yang Fire			癸 Yin Water			壬 Yang Water		
	申 Monkey			丑 Ox			申 Monkey		
	庚 Yang Metal	壬 Yang Water	戊 Yang Earth	己 Yin Earth	癸 Yin Water	辛 Yin Metal	庚 Yang Metal	壬 Yang Water	戊 Yang Earth

The Chinese considered the year 1933 to commence from 4 February 1933. Therefore, 30 January 1933 is calculated as 1932 in the Chinese calendar.

The year 1932 was the year of 壬 Yang Water 申 Monkey. The 壬 Yang Water that he needed had already arrived in his life. Furthermore, there was also 壬 Yang Water inside the 申 Monkey. He was appointed Chancellor on 30 January 1933. This was the day of 丙 Yang Fire 申 Monkey in the month of 癸 Yin Water 丑 Ox. The water was at peak strength in the 丑 Ox month which represented the winter season. There was even more 壬 Yang Water in the 申 Monkey day of his appointment as Chancellor. So his authority was very strong that year.

The year 1933 was the year of the 癸 Yin Water 酉 Rooster. The 酉 Rooster represented mid-autumn season when metal is at peak strength. When metal is strong, wood would be weak. The kindness, if any, was gone. Shortly after his ascension to power, he started to eliminate his rivals by starting concentration camps.

AN ANALYSIS OF HOW THE DARK SIDE BEGAN

In June 1934, he used the SA to murder his political rivals, notably Ernest Roehm. The year 1934 was the year of 甲 Yang Wood 戌 Dog. By then, he had commenced his 癸 Yin Water 亥 Pig luck cycle. The 亥 Pig had a combination with his 寅 Tiger day master which resulted in wood. So if wood represented kindness, why did he commit murder instead of kind acts? The 亥 Pig also had a destruction relationship with the 寅 Tiger. The 壬 Yang Water in the 亥 Pig destroyed the 丙 Yang Fire in the 寅 Tiger. This meant that he would use his authority to eliminate his rivals.

On 16 March 1935, Hitler renounced the Versailles Treaty. Germany embarked on a course of massive rearmament of its armed forces. The year 1935 was the year of 乙 Yin Wood 亥 Pig. The 亥 Pig year had a self-punishment relationship with his 亥 Pig luck cycle. By rearming Germany and preparing for war, he embarked on a course of aggression. This would not be favourable for him or his country in the long run. Later, when he made some serious blunders, it would doom his country to defeat.

Date of first concentration camps 31-7-1941

时Hour?	日Day	月Month	年Year
	庚 Yang Metal	乙 Yin Wood	辛 Yin Metal
	辰 Dragon	未 Goat	巳 Snake
	戊 乙 癸 Yang Yin Yin Earth Wood Water	己 丁 乙 Yin Yin Yin Earth Fire Wood	丙 戊 庚 Yang Yang Yang Fire Earth Metal

In July 1941, after the invasion of Russia had started, Hitler had even more opportunity to fulfil his aims stated in his *"Mein Kampf"*. He authorised more concentration camps to be built to meet "The Final Solution." The year 1941 was the year of 辛Yin Metal 巳Snake. The 巳Snake represented the summer season when fire was strong. However, the 巳Snake also belonged to the metal frame together with the 酉Rooster and the 丑Ox. The metal inside the 巳Snake is strong. The strong metal controlled the wood. When the wood was weak, the kindness was gone. The 巳Snake clashed with his 亥Pig luck cycle. This clash did not bode well for him in the long run.

AN ANALYSIS OF THE BLUNDERS THAT LED TO DEFEAT

Hitler was not born on a wood day. He was a 丙Yang Fire day master. To a fire person, the wood provided the fuel for the fire. Therefore, the wood element represented his resources.

When his 壬Yang Water arrived in the 亥Pig luck cycle from the age of 45, his fortunes improved. He could become the Chancellor. However, the 亥Pig combined with his 寅Tiger day of birth that resulted in wood. This made the strong wood in his birth chart overly strong.

Adolf Hitler Luck Cycle

35	25			15			5
甲 Yang Wood	乙 Yin Wood			丙 Yang Fire			丁 Yin Fire
子 Rat	丑 Ox			寅 Tiger			卯 Rabbit
癸 Yin Water	己 Yin Earth	癸 Yin Water	辛 Yin Metal	甲 Yang Wood	丙 Yang Fire	戊 Yang Earth	乙 Yin Wood

75			65	55			45	
庚 Yang Metal			辛 Yin Metal	壬 Yang Water			癸 Yin Water	
申 Monkey			酉 Rooster	戌 Dog			亥 Pig	
庚 Yang Metal	壬 Yang Water	戊 Yang Earth	辛 Yin Metal	戊 Yang Earth	辛 Yin Metal	丁 Yin Fire	壬 Yang Water	甲 Yang Wood

It was not favourable for his already strong wood to be further strengthened. This situation had two serious consequences. Hitler became too superstitious. He relied too much on his intuition to conduct the war.

The too strong wood meant that he played into the hands of Allied deception many times during the war. The best known instance was the invasion of Normandy on D-Day, 6 June 1944. Hitler refused to release the Panzer divisions to attack the beach heads because he had fallen for the Allied ruse that the main invasion would be launched at Pas de Calais.

The other consequence was his mental breakdown. When the strong wood encountered years when the metal element was strong, the resulting clash made the mental instability worse. After he turned

47 years old in 1936, these years were 1941 (the 辛Yin Metal巳 Snake year) and 1944 (the 甲Yang Wood 申Monkey year).

In 1941, Hitler made two decisions that lost the war. In June 1941, he launched *Operation Barbarossa* to invade the Soviet Union. In December 1941, he declared war on the United States.

On 20 July 1944, Lt.-Col Stauffenberg set off a bomb in the building which Hitler was conducting a meeting. Although Hitler was shielded from the bomb explosion by the massive oak table, he became a physical and mental wreck. He could no longer trust any of his generals. He ranted and raved about the deteriorating military situation. In April 1945, he told General Karl Koller to cease firing his artillery in Berlin as it was deafening him. He refused to accept reality. When he was told in turn that it was the Russian guns that were pounding what was left of Berlin from the Allied air raids to rubble, Hitler refused to believe it.

APPENDIX I:
HITLER'S MENTAL INSTABILITY & INBREEDING

HIS ANCESTRY

The father of Adolf Hitler was Alois Schikelgruber. He was probably born on 7 June 1837 to Maria Anna Schikelgruber in Strones, Austria. But the identity of the father of Alois is not known.

Adolf Hitler was born on a 丙Yang Fire day. His fire was produced by wood which represented his mother. The wood was controlled by the metal, so his father was represented by metal. In turn, his father, Alois, had to be produced by his mother. Since earth produced metal, the mother of Alois (who was Maria Anna Schikelgrubber) was represented by earth. This earth mother (who was also the paternal grandmother to Adolf Hitler) had to be controlled by wood. Therefore, the paternal grandfather of Adolf was represented by wood. To a wood person, the wealth element is represented by earth.

Hitler was born in the spring season when wood was at peak strength. The earth element was weak in spring as it was controlled by the earth element. His paternal grandfather could not have been a wealthy person.

The wood element was in turn controlled by the metal element. The metal element was not strong in the spring season. Adolf Hitler's paternal grandfather was not only poor, he also had no authority.

There were three possible persons who could be the father of Alois Schikelgruber. The first person was Johann Georg Hiedler who was a poor journeyman or mill worker. How poor was he? He was said to be so poor that he did not even own the bed he slept in! During that period in history, there were frequent strikes by the journeymen's association. This meant that Johann Georg was out of work for lengthy periods. If he defied the strike and worked, he would have been blacklisted.

The other possible father was Johann Nepomuk Huetler/ Huttler/Hiedler. He owned the mill that employed Johann Georg and was his brother despite the different surnames.

Five years after Alois Schikelgrubber was born, his mother, Maria Anna, married Johan Georg Hiedler. His mother also sent him to live with Johann Nepomuk Huettler. When Alois was ten years old, his mother died at the age of 52. Johann Nepomuk took care of Alois until he was 13 years old.

This situation has posed many questions for historians. If Johann Georg was the father of Alois, why did Maria Anna wait five years to marry him? If Johann Georg was indeed the father, why give up custody of Alois to Johann Nepomuk?

On the other hand, if Johann Nepomuk was the father of Alois, why did Maria Anna marry the other brother? If Johann Nepomuk was the father, then it might have been galling for Johann Georg to take care of Alois, who was after all, his brother's son. That might explain why the couple gave up custody of Alois to Johann Nepomuk. But it did not explain why they waited five years to do so.

The most probable father of Alois Schikelgruber was Johann Georg who was poor and had no authority.

The third possibility was that Maria Anna was working for a Jewish family known as the Frankenbergers. She could have been made pregnant by one of the sons, Leopold Frankenberger. In an effort to hush up the matter, the Frankenbergers paid her some money as compensation.

The problem with this theory was that there were no Jews living in Graz during this period. They had been banished and did not return until around 1860s, long after Alois was born. Even if the Frankenbergers did exist, this theory implied that they had the money to buy Maria Anna's silence. Since Adolf Hitler's paternal grandfather was poor, then the possible father of Alois Hitler could not have been a Frankenberger.

However, this is only astrological "evidence" which would not be accepted in any court of law. For those who want a more rational approach, they should try the more scientific methods of

DNA. With the passage of time, it is no longer possible to conduct any meaningful DNA tests that can produce satisfactory results acceptable to the majority of scientists and historians.

In early 1939, Hitler ordered General Knittersched to send troops to destroy the village of Dollersheim, Austria where his paternal grandmother's grave was located. He took care to erase any written records of his ancestry. However, some historians such as Werner Maser argued that Dollersheim was destroyed by the Red Army in 1945 under Stalin's orders.

THE INBREEDING IN HIS FAMILY

The issue was not merely trying to identify who his paternal grandfather was. Even if the identity of his paternal grandfather cannot be satisfactorily resolved, there was already sufficient evidence of inbreeding in his family tree. The inbreeding increased the chances of hereditary diseases and probably contributed to Hitler's mental disorders.

It seemed that Maria Anna Schickelgruber married one brother, Johann Georg Hiedler, and had a lover in the other brother, Johann Nepomuk Huettler. This was the first instance of inbreeding.

When Adolf Hitler's father, Alois Hitler married his third wife, Karla Poelzl, they committed the second instance of inbreeding. Karla was the granddaughter of Johann Nepomuk Huettler. It was strange that she called her husband "Uncle Alois".

This inbreeding might have contributed to the weak disposition of the children. Three siblings died of diphtheria in infancy. The other elder sibling, Edmund, died of measles at the age of 16. Only Adolf and Paula lived to adulthood. By comparison, the two children born to the second wife of Alois Hitler, Franziska Maztelberger, lived to adulthood. These were Alois Hitler, Jr. and Angela Hitler who married Leo Raubal. They had a daughter, also known as Angela. When Alois Hitler married his first wife, Anna Glasl-Horer, she was already aged 50 and he was aged 36. No wonder his first wife did not bear him any children!

When Hitler became Chancellor, he had an affair with Angela, better known as Geli, who was the daughter of his step sister, Angela. This was the third instance of inbreeding. Geli fawned on Adolf Hitler and later committed suicide.

It was probable that Hitler was mentally unstable. Doctor Andrew Norman argued in *"Hitler: The Final Analysis"* (Spellmount Publishers, 2007) that Hitler suffered from mental disorder that was genetically caused by inbreeding in his family.

Aytun Altindal was a Turkish writer who wrote a highly unusual work, *"Behind the Mask of Hitler"* (Janus Publishing, 2010). It was part biography, mostly occult history. The usefulness of the work rested on the writer's attempts to trace the ancestry of Hitler.

HIS MENTAL INSTABILITY

In Chinese medicine, the head is represented by 甲Yang Wood and the liver by 乙Yin Wood. Excessive anger is said to be harmful to the liver. Anger may cause a person to suffer from headaches, deafness, hypertension and epilepsy

Hitler's mother had died when she was 47 years old. Hitler was afraid that due to hereditary issues, he might not be able to live beyond 47. From 1936 onwards, he began to show more temper tantrums, delusions of self-grandeur and bouts of self-pity. These were clear signs of paranoia in the final decade of his life.

He refused to choose a competent medical adviser. Heinrich Hoffmann was his photographer. Hoffman recommended Doctor Theo Morell, a skin specialist to Hitler. Like Hitler, Morell also indulged in fantasies and was an inveterate liar.

If Hitler wanted a bad doctor, Theo Morell was the ideal candidate. At that time, Hitler was suffering from eczema on his feet and legs. He had interrupted sleep patterns and gastric problems. He carefully cultivated his public image as a teetotaller and a non-smoker. He avoided any signs of weakness in public, even the wearing of spectacles.

Instead of helping Hitler recover, Theo Morell only made his patient's condition worse during the remaining nine years of Hitler's life.

Hitler believed in *Schicksal* (Destiny), that he was the chosen one to lead Germany out of her malaise. He would call on *Vorsehung* (Providence) when he was unable to make a decision. He believed in the manifestation of the Will as explained by the German philosopher, Arthur Schopenhauer. On 30 April 1945, he wrote his will, naming Admiral Karl Donitz as his successor. Then he made his last decision—to commit suicide with his mistress, Eva Braun, in a bunker in Berlin.

APPENDIX II:
ADOLF HITLER'S PROBABLE FAMILY TREE
(ABRIDGED)

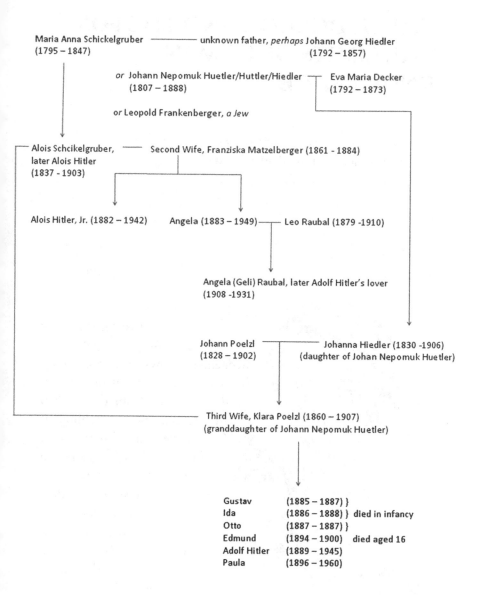

Maria Anna Schickelgruber (1795 – 1847) ———— unknown father, *perhaps* Johann Georg Hiedler (1792 – 1857)

or Johann Nepomuk Huetler/Huttler/Hiedler (1807 – 1888) — Eva Maria Decker (1792 – 1873)

or Leopold Frankenberger, *a Jew*

Alois Schcikelgruber, later Alois Hitler (1837 - 1903) ——— Second Wife, Franziska Matzelberger (1861 - 1884)

Alois Hitler, Jr. (1882 – 1942)   Angela (1883 – 1949) —— Leo Raubal (1879 -1910)

Angela (Geli) Raubal, later Adolf Hitler's lover (1908 -1931)

Johann Poelzl (1828 – 1902) ——— Johanna Hiedler (1830 -1906) (daughter of Johan Nepomuk Huetler)

Third Wife, Klara Poelzl (1860 – 1907) (granddaughter of Johann Nepomuk Huetler)

Gustav	(1885 – 1887) }	
Ida	(1886 – 1888) }	died in infancy
Otto	(1887 – 1887) }	
Edmund	(1894 – 1900)	died aged 16
Adolf Hitler	(1889 – 1945)	
Paula	(1896 – 1960)	

CHAPTER FOUR

THE HEDGEHOG AND THE FOX: THE LIMITS OF HUMAN KNOWLEDGE

"The time to get involved in a science is when it is in a mess . . ."
(Donald Carl Johanson & Maitland Eddy,
"Lucy: The Beginnings of Humankind", 1981)

"The fox knows many things but the hedgehog knows one big thing." This was the fragment of the verse that survived from the work of the Greek poet Archilochus. Foxes have many different ideas or focus on a wide variety of things. Hedgehogs concentrate on one central system or idea.

Isaiah Berlin used this phrase as the title of his book, *"The Hedgehog and the Fox"* (Weidenfeld & Nicholson, 1953). It shall not be necessary to discuss in any detail his essay about Tolstoy's views of world history. Instead, we only wanted to borrow this phrase to show that astrology is only one field of study out of so many possible diverse disciplines that one could study.

We propose to do so by examining the life and achievements of a paleoanthropologist, Donald Carl Johanson. Then we shall look briefly at the unique case of twins, the Shaffer brothers. Finally, we shall consider the spectrum of various astrology studies available to the enthusiast.

Six years later, George Steiner asked his readers to choose between *"Tolstoy or Dostoevsky"* (Faber & Faber, 1959). Perhaps the implication was that if one chose Dostoevsky, then he need not bother with what Tolstoy thought or wrote. Tolstoy was said to have a copy of *"The Brothers Karamazov"* by his side when he died in 1910.

PART I: DONALD CARL JOHANSON

THE DISCOVERY OF "LUCY"

Mention the word "archaeologist" to the layman and the image that he conjured up was probably Indiana Jones searching for lost treasures in the Steven Spielberg movies. Harrison Ford fighting the bad guys and escaping with the treasures or the woman he rescued may make for great action movies. But these are certainly not typical activities for the real life archaeologist or palaeontologist. If they were so busy fighting and evading the villains, they would have no time or peace to search and dig, let alone start excavating once they have found the suitable site.

In late November 1974, Donald Carl Johanson, an American palaeontologist, was a worried man. It was his second season at Hadar, about 100 miles north of Addis Ababa, Ethiopia. His team of 11 scientists had been excavating for about a year. He had been given a grant to finance his work for two years. By the end of the first year, the funds meant for two years were already running low.

He had to find something worthwhile and find it fast to prove that his expedition was worth the financial backing. Otherwise, there might not even be a second year of excavation.

On 30 November 1974, he was tempted to stay back in his tent to categorise the fossils his team had found. Instead, he went out excavating. He later said that he felt that it was his lucky day. He was right—he found the fossils that turned out to be a female hominid, at least 3 million years old, perhaps even more. Johanson labelled his fossils "Lucy" and eventually published his findings with Maitland Edey in *"Lucy: The Beginnings of Humankind"* (Simon & Schuster, 1981).

It was the find of a lifetime that would make Johanson famous. If he had searched at the site a year or two earlier, the strata would not have been sufficiently eroded to expose the fossils. If he had explored a year later, the rains would have washed away the fossils. Johanson pensively reflected that some palaeontologists worked their entire lives without making any significant finds.

THE EARLY YEARS OF STUDY AND STRUGGLE

Donald Carl Johanson was born on 28 June 1943 to Swedish immigrants who settled in Chicago. His father was a barber who died when he was only two years old. His mother then shifted to live in Hartford, Connecticut. He found a surrogate father in Paul Lesser, a neighbour who taught anthropology at the Hartford Seminary Foundation. Johanson showed an early interest in anthropology when he browsed through Lesser's library. By the time he reached high school, he decided to become an anthropologist.

Lesser tried to dissuade him by advising him to study chemistry instead because the financial future of chemists was more secure. Initially, Johanson tried very hard to follow this advice at the University of Illinois. But he found that he tended to hang around the anthropology department more often than the chemistry department. Finally, he gave in to the inevitable and switched to major in anthropology.

After spending several summers in anthropology digs in the American Midwest, he had the temerity to apply to Clark Howells for a travelling scholar program. Howells, then aged 39, had established his reputation in the late 1960s by his finds at the Omo River in southern Ethiopia. He was impressed by the enthusiasm and sincerity that Johanson displayed and agreed to take him on. Johanson worked three seasons with Howells in the field.

THE INVITATION AND THE DILEMMA

By mid-1971, Johanson faced a dilemma. He met Maurice Taieb, a French geologist who invited him to join his next exploration of the Afar Triangle, northern Ethiopia. The Great Rift Valley in Africa consisted of three geological rift systems, resulting in rich geological deposits at places such as Olduvai Gorge and the Afar Triangle. Johanson was then preparing his postgraduate dissertation, had only a little money saved up and no prospects of any teaching job. His marriage, barely two years old, was under strain due to his prolonged absences in the field and his heavy work load. Howells advised him to stay and finish his dissertation, without which he could not get any job or money. But if he did not go, Taieb would certainly ask someone else.

Then he was offered a post to teach anthropology by Case Western Reserve, Cleveland. He really stuck his neck out by asking for an advance of $1,000 for fieldwork in the summer before he could join their faculty in the autumn. To his surprise, Case Western wanted him so badly that they agreed to advance him the money. Johanson scrapped another $600 from his savings and he joined Taieb in Addis Ababa. Taieb managed to extract an exploration permit from the Ethiopian Ministry of Culture. They hired a guide from the Afar tribe and reached the tableland of Hadar. They explored for three days and found pig fossils which were estimated to be about 3 million years old. Taieb, Johanson and Yves Coppens, the French leader of the Omo expedition, agreed to organise a formal expedition by the autumn of 1973.

THE FIRST HADAR SEASON AND THE KNEE JOINTS

During the first Hadar season, Johanson found three knee joints which he identified as hominid. To get confirmation, he flew to Nairobi to show the fossils to Mary and Richard Leakey. They confirmed that the knee joints were hominid, that is, it was a human-like knee joint instead of an ape knee joint.

Then Taieb and Coppens announced their findings of the knee joints to the press in Paris. This was important to palaeontologists so that they could get funding and government support.

Johanson showed the knee joints to Owen Lovejoy, the authority on locomotion and professor of anthropology at Kent State University. Lovejoy confirmed that this hominid was fully bipedal, that is he could run fast on his hind legs. But the hominid was a midget, probably not more than 3 feet tall and had a brain not much larger than a peanut. This finding would upset the established family tree of human ancestors. Lovejoy told Johanson to go back and find the entire family. After Johanson obliged, Lovejoy would later say that "he found Mom and Pop."

THE SECOND HADAR SEASON AND "LUCY"

Johanson could not publish his findings immediately as he had to go back to teach at Cleveland. However, he managed to raise about $25,000 in funds for his next expedition. In the second field season at Hadar, it was Alemayehu Afsaw, the representative from the Ethiopian Ministry of Culture, who found the first hominid lower jaws with molars in it. Later he found two halves of jaws, which when fitted together formed a complete palate with every tooth in position—an extremely rare find. The third jaw was found by the Tigrean workers employed by the expedition.

By then, the funds from the National Science Foundation and the Cleveland backers were running perilously low. When Johanson informed Howells of the find of the jaws, Howells was so excited, he cabled the Leakey Foundation who sent $10,000. This was enough to last the expedition for the remainder of the second Hadar season. On 30 November 1974, Johanson found "Lucy."

Johanson had persuaded James Aronson, a geologist, to join the second Hadar field season. Aronson was an expert on argon-potassium dating methods. After conducting exhaustive tests back at Cleveland, he dated the basalt samples at 3.75 million years old, Lucy and the "First Family" at 3.5 million years, the jaws and the knee joints at 4 million years.

However, finding "Lucy" was easier than getting her fossils out of Ethiopia. The government regulations required them to number the fossils and logged into the National Museum. Then they had to apply to the Antiques Department to get the fossils out. The Museum Director refused to accept the fossils on the grounds that he had no more storage space. After five days of running around, Johanson finally got the Museum to accept the fossils.

By then, the ruler of Ethiopia, Haile Selassie, had fallen from power. The government departments did not dare make independent decisions without instructions from the *Dergue*, the central government. For one week, Johanson pestered for the letter that would release the fossils to him. Exasperated, he finally arranged for a meeting between the Director of Antiques, the Museum Director and other officials. This meeting seemed to start the wheels of officialdom rolling and the Minister agreed to dictate the letter of release.

But the storekeeper had gone out by 5.30 pm and he would stop work at 6 pm, no matter what his bosses might say. To Johanson's relief, the Museum Director helped him to pack the fossils. Then he rushed to the airport and went through Customs. The Customs officials had read of "Lucy" in the newspapers and when they saw the fossils, everyone around them gawked. The next minute, Johanson was waved through Customs and left Ethiopia with his precious "Lucy." It began to dawn on him that perhaps his find might rival that of major paleoanthropologists such as Richard Leakey.

THE THIRD HADAR SEASON AND "THE FIRST FAMILY"

The unstable political situation in Ethiopia cast a shadow on the third Hadar field season from September to December 1975. There was also the possibility of war with neighbouring Eritrea. During this third field season, Mike Bush, a quiet medical doctor who was interested in archaeology, found two hominid premolars. Then Michele, the wife of a French movie team with the expedition, found a large hominid heel bone. This led to further excavations and the haul of a large quantity of hominid bones in what was labelled as the "333 clay layer."

When Johanson showed his fossils to Mary and Richard Leakey, he met Tim White, a palaeontologist who had worked for the Leakeys. After examining the fossils, White said that the Hadar fossils were similar to the fossils found by the Leakeys at Laetoli, near Olduvai Gorge in Tanzania. The Leakey and Johanson fossils were given the name "The First Family" of humankind.

THE FOURTH HADAR SEASON AND THE STONE TOOLS

The fourth Hadar field season almost did not take place. The tense political situation had reduced the Ethiopian civil service to near paralysis. Both the American and French embassies strongly advised Johanson and Taieb not to go. Stories of disappearances and deaths were commonplace.

But the Ethiopian government had only allowed them to keep the fossils for one year after which they had to be returned. Johanson found an expert in casting, Bill McIntosh who had to work under a tight schedule. During the fourth season which ended around December 1976, they unearthed stone tools and a lower jaw complete with all its teeth.

On 29 January 1980, Johanson and Taieb returned about 350 fossils to Mammo Tessema, Keeper of the National Museum, in an elaborate ceremony. Johanson had to return the bones of "Lucy" after five years of study. He later wrote that he felt like a parent giving away a child for adoption.

A BRIEF ANALYSIS OF HIS LIFE

Donald Carl Johanson was born on a 丁Yin Fire day which was seated on the 巳Snake. Inside the巳Snake, there is 丙Yang Fire. That means his丁Yin Fire is already rooted in his巳Snake day. He was born in the 午Horse month. The午Horse month represented mid-summer when fire was at peak strength. His fire is very strong indeed.

Donald Carl Johanson 28-6-1943

时Hour	日Day	月Month	年Year
甲 Yang Wood	丁 Yin Fire	戊 Yang Earth	辛 Yin Metal
辰 Dragon	巳 Snake	午 Horse	未 Goat
戊　　乙　　癸 Yang　Yin　Yin Earth　Wood　Water	丙　　戊　　庚 Yang　Yang　Yang Fire　Earth　Metal	丁　　己 Yin　Yin Fire　Earth	己　　丁　　乙 Yin　Yin　Yin Earth　Fire　Wood

His mother was represented by wood and his father was represented by metal. The metal is found in the Heavenly Stem above his 未Goat year. There are no roots for the metal in his 午Horse month which is the palace for the father. This could indicate that his father is absent, perhaps due to divorce, abandonment of the family or death. The metal element was weak in the summer season so his father's influence or health will be weak. For that matter, the wood element is also weak in summer. He was probably not close to either parent, even if his father had survived to live to an older age.

Since he was born on a巳Snake day and the巳Snake did not clash with the午Horse month, it was less likely that he did not get along with his father. The metal had roots in his巳Snake day so he could have fairly good relationships with his surrogate father.

A person with such a strong fire chart needed the壬Yang Water of the ocean to balance the fire. He also needed 庚Yang Metal.

Johanson already had the庚Yang Metal in his 巳Snake day of birth. He did not have any壬Yang Water in his birth chart.

HIS LUCKY DAY

In 1974, Johanson was aged 31 and in his luck cycle of乙Yin Wood 卯Rabbit. There was no壬Yang Water in the卯Rabbit. It was not even his favourable luck cycle. Yet he discovered Lucy during this period. Was it Fate or human action that brought about the chance discovery?

Donald Carl Johanson Luck Cycle

37	27	17	7
甲 Yang Wood	乙 Yin Wood	丙 Yang Fire	丁 Yin Fire
寅 Tiger	卯 Rabbit	辰 Dragon	巳 Snake
甲 丙 戊 Yang Yang Yang Wood Fire Earth	乙 Yin Wood	戊 乙 癸 Yang Yin Yin Earth Wood Water	丙 戊 庚 Yang Yang Yang Fire Earth Metal

77	67	57	47
庚 Yang Metal	辛 Yin Metal	壬 Yang Water	癸 Yin Water
戌 Dog	亥 Pig	子 Rat	丑 Ox
戊 辛 丁 Yang Yin Yin Earth Metal Fire	壬 甲 Yang Yang Water Wood	癸 Yin Water	己 癸 辛 Yin Yin Yin Earth Water Metal

Although the壬Yang Water that he needed had not arrived, the卯Rabbit represented mid-spring when the wood energy was at its peak. The Heavenly Stem was also乙Yin Wood. This structure indicated the dry wood of small plants. Johanson was born on a 丁 Yin Fire day master. His 丁 Yin Fire needed this dry wood to fuel his fire. In that sense, the 卯 Rabbit luck cycle favoured him even though there was no 壬 Yang Water.

Lucy discovered 30-11-1974

时 Hour	日 Day	月 Month	年 Year
壬 Yang Water	乙 Yin Wood	乙 Yin Wood	甲 Yang Wood
午 Horse	亥 Pig	亥 Pig	寅 Tiger
丁 　 己 Yin 　 Yin Fire 　 Earth	壬 　 甲 Yang 　 Yang Water 　 Wood	壬 　 甲 Yang 　 Yang Water 　 Wood	甲 　 丙 　 戊 Yang 　 Yang 　 Yang Wood 　 Fire 　 Earth

Lucy was discovered on a 亥 Pig day in the 亥 Pig month. The two 亥 Pigs clashed with his 巳 Snake day of birth. Yet he wrote that he felt that it was his lucky day. How could it be his lucky day when there were clashes with his day of birth? But events would prove him right. The 亥 Pig brought him the 壬 Yang Water that he needed. This was a good clash with his 巳 Snake day. Not all the clashes in astrology are bad clashes.

However, even though it may have been a good day, the person concerned still had to take the appropriate action to benefit from it. How did one know what was the appropriate action? That would depend on what were the issues that one was faced with. In Johanson's case, he had a financial crisis which he needed to resolve as soon as possible. The best way to solve it was to find some major fossils. Such a discovery would prove to the financial backers that the expedition was worthwhile and also help to establish Johanson's reputation. In order to make such a find possible, he had to go out to the site instead of remaining in camp to do background work.

PART II: THE SHAFFER TWINS

Anthony and Peter Shaffer were twin brothers born within five minutes of each other. Since they were born on the same day and hour, it seemed logical that they should share the same destinies. But did they? Both of them had successful careers as screenwriters and often collaborated in their work. Peter seemed to be more famous as a playwright than Anthony who found his niche as a screenwriter.

Probably his best known play was *"Amadeus."*. In the opening scenes of the 1984 movie version of this play, the first movement of Mozart's Symphony No. 25 in G minor, K 183 can be heard. This music is both macabre and melancholic. It was a suitable motif to show the scenes of the inmates in the insane asylum to which the composer Antonio Salieri had been confined in his last years.

Tom Hulce played the role of Mozart who was reduced to a giggling, irresponsible and playful child. But it was F. Murray Abraham who stole the show with his brilliant rendition of the ageing, embittered Salieri. If he had the first scenes, then he also hogged the final scenes with his cry of "Mediocrity, I absolve thee!" For his pains, he was awarded a well-deserved Oscar.

Peter Shaffer indulged in artistic licence when he hinted that Mozart's death was due to poisoning. None of the leading Mozart scholars such as H.C. Robbins Landon, Alfred Einstein or Eric Blom found any historical evidence that Mozart was poisoned, let alone poisoned by Salieri.

Anthony and Peter Shaffer 15-5-1926

时 Hour	日 Day	月 Month	年 Year
己 Yin Earth	甲 Yang Wood	癸 Yin Water	丙 Yang Fire
巳 Snake	辰 Dragon	巳 Snake	寅 Tiger
丙　戊　庚 Yang Yang Yang Fire Earth Metal	戊　乙　癸 Yang Yin Yin Earth Wood Water	丙　戊　庚 Yang Yang Yang Fire Earth Metal	甲　丙　戊 Yang Yang Yang Wood Fire Earth

The Shaffer brothers were born on a 甲 Yang Wood day in the 巳 Snake month. As the 巳 Snake represented summer, wood was weak because the wood had been used to fuel the fire. However, the wood in their charts is not that weak. The wood is rooted in their 辰 Dragon day of birth and their 寅 Tiger year.

They needed 癸 Yin Water, 庚 Yang Metal and 丁 Yin Fire. The 癸 Yin Water symbolised the rain water to nourish their wood. The 庚 Yang Metal was needed to chop down their big tree to make it useful.

There was 癸 Yin Water and 庚 Yang Metal in their birth charts. They would have the potential for achievement in their lives.

Anthony Shaffer died on 6 November 2001. If the twin brothers were born on the same day, they should share the same fate. How to explain why one brother died on that day while the other brother survived? Sometimes astrology cannot hope to explain everything. One must be wary of the dangers of over analysis. We cannot ignore the factor of human choice that can make a difference to a given situation.

Here was an ideal birth chart complete with the hour of birth. Yet it would be difficult for any astrologer to analyse the charts. Why?

Despite their fame and successes, there remains a dearth of biographical data about the Shaffer brothers. To date, there has been no biography written about them. The meagre information available online about them is too sketchy and is usually limited to only a list of their works.

Where are the details that matter in a normal person's life? For instance, who were their parents? What was their childhood like? Did they marry and if so, did the marriage last? Did the marriage produce any offspring? If they did not marry, then did they have any romances and if so, with whom and when?

What is the point that we are trying to make? It could be argued that if the chart was complete with birth hour, then any competent astrologer could make his deductions from the chart *per se*. To a certain extent, that may be true. But this argument did not take into account the human factor. Although the birth chart may be fixed, the decisions made by the person during his lifetime are not. Different decisions made by either twin could take him along a different path in life. The Shaffer brothers may have been twins but their lives were not the same in all respects.

PART III: "THE SUMMING UP"

At the age of 64, Somerset Maugham wrote *"The Summing Up"* in 1938. Perhaps he did not expect to live much longer. In the event, he died in 1965 at the age of 91. Likewise, we also need to sum up our work.

There are at least six major types of astrology being practised in the world today. These astrological systems are—in no particular order of importance—Western astrology, Arabic, Judaic, Vedic, Tibetan and Chinese. The last mentioned, Chinese astrology can be subdivided into two schools of astrology. These are the Four Pillars of Destiny (*Ba Zi* which is literally translated as "Eight Characters") and Purple Star astrology *(Zi Wei Do Shu)*.

Perhaps all this goes to show that astrology is alive and well in the world today. In addition, there also exists "dead" astrology such as Egyptian astrology. The astrology is said to be "dead" in the same sense that some languages are dead—because not enough people speak them so the languages die out. In the case of Egyptian astrology, not enough people practise this school of astrology. There are practical reasons not to do so. To begin with, the Egyptian planetary tables do not exist or are hard to come by. It is also difficult to find any book that explained in detail how the Egyptian calendar was derived and how it can be converted to the modern Georgian or Chinese solar-lunar calendar. If these issues were not resolved, how could any enthusiast profess to practise Egyptian astrology, even though it may have its own merits?

Readers who want to delve more deeply into the subject may refer to *"The Complete Astrological Handbook for the 21st Century"* compiled by Anistatia Miller and Jared Brown (Schocken Books, 1999).

The subject of Egyptian astrology is so esoteric that there are only a handful of books on the subject. One such book was *"Egyptian Birth Signs: The Secrets of the Ancient Egyptian Horoscope"* by Storm Constantine (Thorsons, 2002).

Why did we mention the different types of astrology? We began our article by mentioning the hedgehog and the fox. Whatever method of astrology that one may practise, let us not forget that there are also other methods of astrology that may be just as valid and has its own merits. We should not get so engrossed in our own field of astrological studies that we become hedgehogs and forget about the foxes that live on the same planet.

THE PROBLEM OF "EVIDENCE"

In palaeoanthropology, the evidence is usually incomplete. After five years of work, they only managed to find about 60 per cent of "Lucy". Yet this incomplete evidence was accepted by the scientific community and endlessly debated upon. But the origins of Man are not necessarily the origins of Life. The earliest life forms could be simple amoeba that existed long before Man even began to appear.

If palaeoanthropology looked back on the past, then astronomers could choose to look forwards to the future or turn towards the past. They could speculate about the possible end of the sun and the universe. Or they could try to trace the beginnings of Time and the universe. Despite all the scientific equipment and technology available to the modern astronomer—compared to the primitive astronomer in classical Greece or the era of Galileo—the observations made by them remain speculative and cannot be conclusively proven to the satisfaction of everyone that mattered in the scientific community. It was not possible for astronomers to try and bring back samples of soil from the moon or Mars for examination until space travel became a reality. Despite this lack of tangible evidence, astronomers continue to debate based on what is largely intangible evidence.

These are ironies in the scientific world. Scientists work on the axiom that one forms a hypothesis, then tests it by observation and experimentation until the hypothesis is proven. The scientist is supposed to be objective, unlike the artist who has the luxury of indulging in emotions when expressing his art.

But what constitutes "evidence"? The evidence from fossils in the past will always be incomplete. Even with the technology of modern space travel, some soil samples can only be collected from the nearest planets. The vast distances in astronomy are measured in light years but light years exist only as concepts. The distance of a light year is so immense that one cannot physically measure it.

If the scientific world can accept incomplete evidence, why can't the astrologer accept incomplete birth charts? After all, the astrologer is not a scientist. His standard of "evidence" is probably far lower than that required by scientists.

It is not likely that we would ever have enough evidence in whatever discipline that one practised. If he waited for sufficient evidence to publish his findings, the work would never get done. We have to press on regardless of inadequate evidence. The job of the astrologer is no longer confined to *"in futurum videre"* ("to see into the future"). If one chose to do research in astrology, he also had to peer into the past, like the palaeontologist.

Samuel Butler summed it up succinctly when he observed that "Life is the art of drawing sufficient conclusions from insufficient evidence."

CHAPTER FIVE

"ONCE UPON A TIME" SERGIO LEONE REMADE THE WESTERN

"When you want to shoot, shoot . . . . don't talk."
(Eli Wallach's line as Tuco in *"The Good, the Bad and the Ugly"*, 1966)

I f Sergio Leone had not directed his four Western movies, his name would probably have been forgotten today—or at least, not known outside the circles of Italian cinema.

He directed his first movie in 1961 at the age of 32. When he died of heart failure at the age of 60 in 1989, he was working on his next movie based on the siege of Leningrad. This gave him an active working period of about 28 years. Despite all this activity, the public identified his work only from his four spaghetti Westerns and one gangster movie, *"Once upon a time in America."*

THE MIRACLE BABY

Sergio Leone was born on 3 January 1929, the only child of Vincenzo Leone and Edvige Valcarenghi. When he was born, his parents considered his birth as a miracle. His mother was aged 43 and his father aged 50. His mother had given up hope of ever having any children.

His father studied law at the University of Naples. In 1905, he joined a theatre company and began acting under the stage name of Roberto Roberti. His mother was a stage actress who performed under the name Bice Walerian. When she met Vincenzo in 1912, she was already engaged to her fiancé, Prince Walerian. She broke off the engagement and married Vincenzo in 1916. She retired from the stage one year later.

His father retired in 1949 at the age of 70 to live in his home town of Torella dei Lombardi. He died a decade later in 1958. Leone regretted that his father did not live long enough to see his success.

Leone recalled that his first visit to the cinema was around 1939 when he was 10. At that time, the Italian cinemas were full of Hollywood movies—all dubbed in Italian. He was exposed to the films of John Ford, Anthony Mann and Nicholas Ray espousing the American virtues of justice, loyalty and honour.

WHEN ITALY MET AMERICA

In 1943, the German armies began to occupy Italy. Leone wanted to join the partisans to fight them. His mother begged him not to take the risk. She had been married for 13 years before giving birth to her only child at an advanced age. She could not bear the thought of losing her only child. She suffered a stroke in in the late 1950s and could not communicate with her son. She died in 1969 at the age of 83. Sergio Leone adored his father but felt distant from his mother.

On 10 July 1943, the Allies invaded Sicily. By 3 September 1943, Montgomery's Eighth Army had crossed the Straits of Messina to Italy. Six days later, General Mark Clark's Fifth Army followed by landing at Salerno. After a hard slugfest against Field Marshal Kesselring's stout defences, General Clark finally entered Rome at the head of his 88th Division on 4 June 1944. At that time, Leone was only 14 years old.

The Italian audiences had been fed a steady diet of American films. They adored Gary Cooper, Errol Flynn, James Cagney and Charlie Chaplin playing the American hero on the screen chasing the American dream of freedom and opportunity. Instead, when the Americans arrived in Italy, the Italians found them to be materialistic and possessive, with no hesitation about flooding the black market with their goods. Like many other Italian adolescents of his era, Leone was disillusioned.

THE SOCERER'S APPRENTICE

Leone began work in the film industry in his late teens in various positions, usually as an assistant in the second unit. In the late 1950s, he also worked as a screenwriter but was usually not given the credit for his work.

In 1959, he directed his first movie by accident. During the shooting of *"The Last Days of Pompeii" ("Gli Ultimi Giorini di Pompei")*, the director, Mario Bonnard became sick. As Leone was then assistant director, the studio told him to take over as director for the remaining half of the film. But he received no credit for his pains.

In 1961, he directed his first full length movie, *"The Colossus of Rhodes" ("Il Colosso di Rodi")*. But it was just another Roman epic that Italian cinema was churning out at that time.

THE SPAGHETTI WESTERNS

In 1964, he made *"A Fistful of Dollars' ("Per un pugno di dollari")*. It was based on Akira Kurosawa's *"Yojimbo."* Kurosawa was not happy and filed a legal suit.

Leone wanted to hire Henry Fonda and Charles Bronson, his favourite stars. Henry Fonda's agent declined the offer without even bothering to inform Fonda himself. Charles Bronson took one look at the script and declined.

Sergio Leone was persuaded to watch one episode of *"Rawhide"*. When he saw Clint Eastwood acting, he was impressed. He saw that Eastwood could be idle and indifferent like a coiled snake one moment. Then Eastwood would uncoil himself and spring into action the next moment, usually in some action scenes such as fighting the villains.

At that time Eastwood had finished one season of *"Rawhide"* and was taking a break before the next season started. When he was told of Leone's offer, he thought that a paid vacation in Italy with his wife would suit him fine.

But he had a shock when he met Leone. He found out that Leone could not speak English and he could not speak Italian. They had to communicate through interpreters who were not always available. Leone would typically tell his foreign actors to watch him while he acted out a scene. He expected the actors to act like what he did when the cameras began shooting. After Eastwood read the script, he felt that his role would be enhanced if his dialogue was reduced. In doing so, he became one of the few actors who wanted less lines of dialogue.

As it turned out, *"A Fistful of Dollars"* would be the movie that launched the career of Clint Eastwood. It was also the first of trilogy of Westerns that Sergio Leone would make. He would follow up the success with *"For a Few Dollars More"* (*"Per qualche dollaro in piu"*) in 1965. But this time Lee van Cleef would be given a lead role opposite Eastwood.

In 1966, Leone made *"The Good, the Bad and the Ugly"* (*"Il buono, il brutto, il cattivo"*) about three characters caught up in the US Civil War. The lead roles were played by Clint Eastwood, Eli Wallach and Lee van Cleef. Although Eastwood played *"The Good"* hero, the central character was *"The Ugly"* played by Eli Wallach. Both of them faced off *"The Bad"* played by Eli Wallach during a triangular shootout in the climatic showdown at the Cemetery.

By the end of this movie, Clint Eastwood had enough of working with Leone and returned to the US. He eventually became a director and actor in movies such as his *"Dirty Harry"* series.

After the commercial success of his *"Dollars"* trilogy, Charles Bludhorn of Paramount Pictures was interested enough to offer Leone a budget of $1 million to make his next Western. In 1969, Leone directed his sprawling epic, *"Once upon a time in the West"* (*"C'era una volta il West"*).

He could finally afford to hire the stars he wanted, Henry Fonda and Charles Bronson. It was typical of Leone to reverse the roles offered to these actors. Fonda was usually given the roles of the hero. Bronson's rugged features meant that he usually played the mean villains. In this movie, Fonda was the villain who hanged Bronson's brother and wanted the land that belonged to Claudia Cardinale. Bronson played the hero who thwarted Fonda's plans to buy the land and wanted revenge for his brother's death.

Leone also wanted his trio of lead actors, Clint Eastwood, Lee van Cleef and Eli Wallach to act in the opening scenes when the three of them would be killed in a shootout with Charles Bronson. Two of the actors, Lee van Cleef and Eli Wallach, agreed. But Clint Eastwood declined. So that was the end of that idea. Eastwood's refusal meant that *"The Man with No Name"* would not die on the screen.

Leone had made four Westerns in six years. After every movie, he always said that he would never make another Western. Yet, by continuing to make one Western after another, he had redefined how the Western could be made—outside the Hollywood tradition set by masters of the genre such as John Ford, Anthony Mann, Henry Hathaway, Howard Hawks and John Sturges.

If Leone was given a budget of $1 million for *"Once upon a time in the West"*, it was a paltry sum compared to the $70 million budget for the next movie based on the 2 ½ year siege of Leningrad during the war. He planned the opening scenes to be played with the music of Shostakovich in the background—the "Leningrad" Symphony No. 10 in E minor. But he never got to make the movie.

On the morning of 30 April 1989, Sergio Leone and his wife Carla were in bed watching television. Sergio leaned his head against her shoulder and said he did not feel well. She called for an ambulance but he was already dead of heart failure before it arrived.

HIS FAMILY AND CHARACTER ANALYSED

Sergio Leone was born on a 戊Yang Earth 申Monkey day in the 子Rat month. The 子Rat month symbolised the peak of winter. The strongest element in winter is water and the weakest element is fire. Fire is required to produce earth. When fire is weak, earth must be weak. Therefore, Leone is a weak earth person. As if that were not enough, his 申 Monkey day has a Three Harmony relationship with his 辰Dragon year and both his 子Rat month and hour that resulted in water. The strong water in winter is thus made even stronger by this relationship.

Sergio Leone 3-1-1929

时Hour	日Day			月Month	年Year		
壬 Yang Water	戊 Yang Earth			甲 Yang Wood	戊 Yang Earth		
子 Rat	申 Monkey			子 Rat	辰 Dragon		
癸 Yin Water	庚 Yang Metal	壬 Yang Water	戊 Yang Earth	癸 Yin Water	戊 Yang Earth	乙 Yin Wood	癸 Yin Water

In theory, earth is said to control water. But there are exceptions to the rule. If the water is too strong, it can wash away earth as in the case of a river overflowing its banks. Since his earth is already weak due to the absence of fire to produce the earth, the overly strong water does not bode well for him.

The water element represented his money. There is water in his 申 Monkey day, 子Rat month and hour and his辰Dragon year. A person who has too many wealth stars in his chart will not become rich. Instead, he will have to struggle to earn a livelihood.

The water is too strong and threatened to wash away his earth. The overly strong water indicated that he had health problems. If he were to encounter even more water in his luck cycles, it was possible that he might even lose his life. But there is also an upside. The strong water meant that this person was imaginative and creative.

He badly needed the 丙Yang Fire which represented sunlight to warm his chart. He also needed 甲Yang Wood to loosen his 戊Yang Earth which was frozen under the winter snow. He only has the 甲 Yang Wood in his birth chart. The 甲Yang Wood was located in the Heavenly Stem above his 子Rat month. When he encountered the 丙Yang Fire in his luck cycle, his fortunes will improve.

There is not a single spark of fire in his chart. Some masters of astrology have argued that one must have both fire and water in the birth chart in order to have any achievement in life. The rationale was that fire and water were polarities. Although fire and water opposed each other, both of them were required. How could one understand joy if there was no sorrow? If there was north, there had to be south.

If this was the case, then how to explain why Leone became famous in his life? He directed many movies in his lifetime but his reputation rested on only a handful of movies—four Western movies and one gangster movie. When we analyse his career, we shall find that his movies succeeded when the fire element arrived in his annual pillars or his luck cycles.

Why was he closer to his father than to his mother who adored her only child?

His mother was represented by fire and his father was represented by water. Since there is no fire in the chart, it could be interpreted to mean that his mother figure was absent or had little or no influence over him. Even if there were any fire in the Heavenly Stems, the fire would have no roots in his 甲Monkey day, 子Rat hour and month and his 辰Dragon year.

If the fire was absent, the water was plentiful and strong in winter. This could mean that he was influenced by his father or was closer to his father.

HIS CAREER ANALYSED

Leone made his first Western, *"A Fistful of Dollars"* in 1964 and was promptly sued by Akira Kurosawa for copying his *"Yojimbo."*

At that time, Leone was a struggling, unknown director in Italy, a country which had directors and films in abundance. Why did he face the legal suit in that year?

The year 1964 was the year of the 甲 Yang Wood 辰 Dragon. Leone was then aged 35 and in his luck cycle of 戊 Yang Earth 辰 Dragon. The relationship between the two 辰 Dragons is said to be that of "self-punishment." What is being punished? The 戊 Yang Earth in the 辰 Dragons represents friends or competitors to Leone. The 癸 Yin Water in the 辰 Dragons represent money to Leone. The 乙 Yin Wood represented legitimate authority such as a trade association or a regulating body. This indicated that some competitor might claim for damages or compensation from Leone.

Sergio Leone Luck Cycle

31	21	11	1
戊 Yang Earth	丁 Yin Fire	丙 Yang Fire	乙 Yin Wood
辰 Dragon	卯 Rabbit	寅 Tiger	丑 Ox
戊 乙 癸 Yang Yin Yin Earth Wood Water	乙 Yin Wood	甲 丙 戊 Yang Yang Yang Wood Fire Earth	己 癸 辛 Yin Yin Yin Earth Water Metal

71	61	51	41
壬 Yang Water	辛 Yin Metal	庚 Yang Metal	己 Yin Earth
申 Monkey	未 Goat	午 Horse	巳 Snake
庚 壬 戊 Yang Yang Yang Metal Water Earth	己 丁 乙 Yin Yin Yin Earth Fire Wood	丁 己 Yin Yin Fire Earth	丙 戊 庚 Yang Yang Yang Fire Earth Metal

Leone was born on a 申Monkey day. He was then in his 辰 Dragon luck cycle and 1964 was also the辰Dragon year. The辰 Dragon luck cycle and year had a Three Harmony relationship with Leone's申Monkey day and 子Rat month. This hinted that the legal dispute could reach an agreement. Leone could continue with shooting his film. If his first movie of what would become the "Dollars Trilogy" had been derailed, it was conceivable that he might not have made his second spaghetti Western.

In 1965, he released the second Western, *"For A Few Dollars More"*. This was the year of the 乙Yin Wood 巳Snake. There is the 丙Yang Fire that Leone needed inside the巳Snake. The arrival of this丙Yang Fire boded well for his second Western.

In 1966, Leone filmed the last Western in his trilogy, *"The Good, The Bad and the Ugly"*. This was the year of丙Yang Fire 午 Horse. The丙Yang Fire in the Heavenly Stem above the午Horse meant that his good fortune could still continue. This丙Yang Fire was rooted in the午Horse which represented summer.

When he made his next movie, *"Once Upon a Time in the West"* in 1969, he ran out of the丙Yang Fire that he needed. This was the year of 巳Yin Earth 酉Rooster. There was no fire at all inside the酉Rooster. His last Western was panned by the critics. Later, it acquired a cult following. This put Leone on the same pedestal with Sam Peckinpah's *"The Wild Bunch"* released in 1969.

But he was not a confident person. Instead, he was tormented by self-doubts. He always thought that the movie he had just finished would be his last. After the previous movie had been finished, he always seemed uncertain in which direction he should turn next. For all his apparent success, he was like a child once his work was over.

This characteristic can be explained by the fact that his chart did not have any fire. One of the attributes of fire was to give a person courage and confidence in life. The absence of fire meant that the person would lack self-confidence all his life.

The酉Rooster had a combination relationship with his 辰 Dragon luck cycle that resulted in metal. The metal element represented his productivity.

When he entered his 巳 Snake luck cycle in 1970 from the age of 41, his favourable period should have begun. The 巳 Snake brought the 丙 Yang Fire that he needed. But he had already made the four Westerns that would establish his reputation before this period. He did not produce or direct any memorable movies during this decade. How to explain why he had already completed his main body of works before the favourable luck cycle started?

The 巳 Snake luck cycle may have brought the 丙 Yang Fire that should have been favourable to him. But the 巳 Snake luck cycle had an ungrateful punishment relationship with his 甲 Monkey day master. The 巳 Snake also had a combination relationship with the 甲 Monkey that resulted in water. As Leone already had too much water in his birth chart, the presence of more water did not augur well for him.

During this decade, he did not make any memorable movies. In 1971, he made his next movie, *"A Fistful of Dynamite"* which was released as *"Duck, You Sucker"* in the US. This movie, which was set during the Mexican Revolution, showed Rod Steiger and James Coburn blowing up practically everything in sight. The movie bombed in the US. The only other memorable movie he produced was *"My Name Is Nobody"* starring Terence Hill and Henry Fonda. Most of the other movies he made during this period were commercials.

From the age of 51, he was in his 庚 Yang Metal 午 Horse luck cycle. The 午 Horse represented summer so he should still have the fire that he needed. However, the 午 Horse luck cycle clashed with his 子 Rat hour of birth.

By the age of 51, the 丙 Yang Fire was gone. He was now in his 午 Horse luck cycle. The 午 Horse represented mid-summer so there was still fire during this period. But the fire inside the 午 Horse is 丁 Yin Fire instead of 丙 Yang Fire. He could still enjoy some fame. But his best period was over.

HIS SUDDEN DEATH

Why did he die a sudden death from natural causes? He died on a 庚Yang Metal 申Monkey day in the辰Dragon month. Since the 辰Dragon month represented spring, wood was strong and metal was weak. The wood element was strong during the spring season. This strong wood controlled his earth similar to the roots of a tree gripping the soil.

Sergio Leone death 30-4-1989

时Hour	日Day	月Month	年Year
丁 Yin Fire	庚 Yang Metal	戊 Yang Earth	己 Yin Earth
丑 Ox	申 Monkey	辰 Dragon	巳 Snake
己　　癸　　辛 Yin　　Yin　　Yin Earth　Water　Metal	庚　　壬　　戊 Yang　Yang　Yang Metal　Water　Earth	戊　　乙　　癸 Yang　　Yin　　Yin Earth　Wood　Water	丙　　戊　　庚 Yang　Yang　Yang Fire　Earth　Metal

However, upon closer examination of the chart, we find that metal was plentiful during the day of his death. There was metal inside the 丑Ox hour, the申Monkey day and the 巳Snake year. There was also 庚Yang Metal in the Heavenly Stem above the申 Monkey day of death. The presence of so much metal exhausted his weak 戊Yang Earth day master.

Then the巳Snake year had a combination relationship with his 申Monkey day of death and also his 申Monkey day of birth that resulted in water. He already had too much water in his birth chart. It was not favourable for him to encounter more water. Too much water threatened to wash away his weak earth. An analogy might be the case of an overflowing river that burst through its earth banks.

This did not necessarily mean that Leone was fated to die on that day. It merely indicated that this would be a difficult day for him. If he could overcome the obstacles on that day, he might live to see another day. Unfortunately, he did not.

"SOMETHING TO DO WITH DEATH": THE REMAKING OF THE WESTERN

How did Leone remake the Western?

Towards the final segment of *"Once upon a time in the West"*, Cheyenne (played by Jason Robards) told Jill McBain (Claudia Cardinale) "You don't understand. People like him (referring to the character Harmonica, played by Charles Bronson) have something inside . . . something to do with death."

No wonder Sir Christopher Frayling chose this line as the title of his book, *"Sergio Leone: Something to do with Death"* (University of Minnesota Press, 2000) which became the definitive biography of Sergio Leone. He followed it up with a study of Leone and the Italian spaghetti Western in *"Sergio Leone: Once upon a time in Italy"* (Thames and Hudson, 2008).

Every scene that Leone shot had to be an epic. He needed 2,000 extras just to shoot a scene. Sometimes, he dwelled too long on silences and close up of faces. These traits caused him to go over the budget and made his films too long. When the studios insisted on cutting his films, the net effect sometimes seemed disjointed.

In the Hollywood Westerns, the hero was typically clean shaven. He rode into town on his sturdy horse, saw someone being bullied or beaten, intervened and rescued the victim, typically a female who might later fall for him. In Leone's movies, the hero was unshaven, wore dirty clothes made dusty by the desert, rode into town on a mule, saw someone being harassed—and continued his journey into town.

There were the close-ups, especially of the eyes. The Italians believed that the eyes revealed everything. When the camera showed a close-up of Clint Eastwood's eyes, they revealed—nothing. The Man with No Name did not give anything away, not even by his expressionless eyes.

There were the lengthy periods of silence, punctuated by sudden bursts of activity such as gunfights. As our essay is not intended to offer a detailed assessment of Sergio Leone's work, two examples will have to suffice.

In the first five minutes of *"The Good, the Bad and the Ugly"*, two gunmen face a third gunman as if they intended to draw their guns against each other. The two of them walked towards the third gunman who also started to walk towards them. When they met, they drew their guns without a word and dashed inside a hut to kill their man. The glass of the window shattered as the Ugly man, played by Eli Wallach, jumped out and escaped on a horse. He left behind one seriously injured and two dead gunmen. There is no dialogue at all. The only sounds heard were the natural sounds such as doors creaking, wind blowing tumbleweeds or water dripping from the windmill.

The first ten minutes of the opening scenes of *"Once upon a time in the West"* are played out mostly in silence. The only dialogue was from the elderly, toothless stationmaster who offered to sell the three men (standing in various doorways) train tickets without their asking for it. Woody Strode hauled the hapless stationmaster to be locked up in a nearby room. The three men settled down to wait for the train to bring the man they came to kill.

The water dripped from the ceiling on Woody Strode's bald head. The third villain, (uncredited actor), pressed his knuckles together. A fly hovered around Jack Elam's lower face. The train arrived and stopped but no passengers disembarked. The silence was broken when a guard opened the sliding door of the only goods wagon in the train to throw down a parcel.

As the trio turned to go away, a harmonica was heard playing. Their intended victim, played by Charles Bronson, had alighted on the opposite side of the tracks. The dialogue between Charles Bronson and Jack Elam consisted of only three brief lines. In the ensuing gunfight, the three villains are killed. The dominant themes in these scenes were silence and close-up of the faces. These themes would be repeated throughout the three hours of the film.

Vincenzo Leone was a scriptwriter who worked with Sergio Leone on his "Dollars" trilogy. Vincenzo said that "with Sergio, every scene had to be an epic." If Sergio Leone had become a musical composer instead of a director, he would have failed miserably. In the composition of music, one does not emphasize every single note of music.

Sergio Leone had long admired the work of Charlie Chaplin. In turning his Westerns into Symphonies of Silence, he paid Chaplin the highest tribute possible.

CHAPTER SIX
WHEN FAME BECAME A BURDEN: THE REAL "LAWRENCE OF ARABIA"

"All men dream, but not equally . . . . the dreamers of the day are dangerous men, for they may act their dream with open eyes, to make it possible."
(T.E. Lawrence, *"Seven Pillars of Wisdom"*, 1923)

*T*o most people, fame would be considered an integral part of their success. When an actor or singer has become famous, he can demand higher fees or royalty from the studio. A politician needed to have fame and popularity to win elections as well as authority to stay in power.

Thomas Edward Lawrence became famous as *"Lawrence of Arabia"* when he helped the Arabs to defeat the Turks in Syria during 1917-1918. Five years later, he tried to forget his fame and enlisted in the RAF under a false name. That was when he found his fame had become a burden. The media got on to his antics. He was forced to leave the RAF to evade the press. Then he joined the Tank Corps under an assumed name but found he was not happy there. He tried to reenlist in the RAF to no avail. When he threatened to commit suicide, Trenchard, the chief of the RAF had to relent. He re-joined the RAF under a false name. But the media was not so easily thrown off the scent.

Surely, this situation was against the norm. After he had become famous, why did he find fame to be a burden instead of an asset?

THE EARLY OBSCURE YEARS

Thomas Edward Lawrence was the second of five sons. His father was Thomas Robert Tighe Chapman, an Irishman who had private means. His first wife had borne him four daughters in Ireland. But his marriage was unhappy. Instead, he fell in love with the nanny who had been employed to look after his children. After the affair became known, he preferred to leave his first wife and adopted the surname of his partner, "Lawrence." He settled down at Dinard, Scotland, with his mistress to raise their family. Despite the illegitimacy of the children, the family was close and harmonious. The father was wealthy so the family was not in material need.

In 1910, Lawrence graduated from Oxford University with honours in Modern History. He had known Janet Laurie since his childhood days. When he proposed, she declined as she seemed more interested in his brother, Will.

In the autumn of 1910, he joined an archaeological excavation at Carchemish, near Jerablus in Syria. The expedition was led by DG Hogarth, the director of the Asmolean Museum to excavate the pottery and other monuments from the lost Hittite city buried at Carchemish. Lawrence was given the task of photography as well as the hiring and managing of the Arab workforce. In the process, he learnt Arabic. He also formed friendships with Leonard Woolley who took over as leader from the second season and with Dahoum, an intelligent Arab youth, from whom he learnt much about the Arab mentality. The years spent with the expedition from 1911 to 1914 were the happiest years of his life. In June 1914, the expedition returned to England after their seventh season in the field. But the outbreak of the First World War in August terminated their work.

In early 1914, Lawrence and Woolley were asked by Captain Newcombe of the Royal Engineers to join a survey party. They surveyed the Sinai Peninsula which was then under Turkish control. Lawrence explored the inland area of Akaba. He did not know it then but in 1917 he would lead the Arab Revolt to attack Akaba. He also learnt about map making and geology. He had long been interested in setting up a printing press to print fine books similar to those made by William Morris. Now he put this interest to good use in making maps. These skills made it inevitable that he would be recruited by Military Intelligence, Cairo in December 1914.

THE YEARS OF WAR

To the British government in Cairo, the immediate aim was to try and defeat the Turks in Syria. But Lawrence also wanted the Arabs to be given self-autonomy. He realised that the Arabs had long been resentful of Turkish rule. If the Turks were defeated, he hoped that the French would be prevented from resuming her colonial empire. But the British government was only concerned in defending the Suez Canal and had no interest in Arab nationalism. As the focus was on the war in the Western Front, the issues in the Middle East were considered a side show. Besides the French, the British government in India also hoped to colonise the fertile land of Mesopotamia after the war.

The outcome of all these concerns resulted in an agreement between Sir Henry McMahon and Sheriff Hussein of Mecca. The McMahon-Hussein agreement gave the Arabs the impression that the British would grant them self-government if they helped to fight the Turks

About the same time and unknown to the British at Cairo, Sir Mark Sykes negotiated with Francois Georges-Picot. The Sykes-Picot agreement gave the British the assurance that they could support the Arab revolt against the Turks without offending the French.

The French believed that they were allowed to resume their colonial empire in Syria and other Arab countries after the war.

In June 1916, Sheriff Hussein led a rebellion against the Turks and captured Mecca, Jidda and Rabegh. The Turks retreated to Medina which was the hub of the Hedjaz Railway, the only rail track linking Damascus to Medina and other cities in the area. But the rebels were poorly armed and would not be able to withstand any counter-offensive by the Turks. Due to the urgency of the situation, Lawrence was sent to Jidda to find out about the situation on the ground.

In October 1916, Lawrence arrived at Sheriff Hussein's camp. He recognised that the rebellion had to spread to the far north if the Arabs hope for self-government was to be realized. He also knew that they had to capture the northern cities of Homs, Homma, Damascus and Aleppo. These cities were between 850 and 1,000 miles from Jidda. There seemed no likelihood that the rebellion could spread so far. Sheriff Hussein was too old to lead his troops in the field. He was respected in the Hedjaz but had no authority in distant Syria where these cities lay. The next leader would have to be chosen among his four sons. Lawrence found the third son, Feisal who was then aged 31 to be the most suitable candidate.

The fishing village of Akaba was located in the Sinai Peninsula, facing the Red Sea. Behind it lay the narrow gorges of the Wadi Itm which led to the nearby mountain town of Maan. Lawrence planned to attack Akaba by an inland detour thereby bypassing the heavily defended Wadi Itm gorges. In July 1917, he led the Arabs in a successful foray that captured Akaba. The Arab occupation of Akaba threatened to cut off the supplies along the Hedjaz Railway from the north to the Turkish garrison at Medina.

By then, General Edmund Allenby had arrived to take over the Egyptian Expeditionary Force. He acknowledged that the Arabs could assist his forces by harassing the Turks in Syria. To achieve this purpose, the British would provide money and supplies to Emir Feisal and his forces. The Arab Revolt had grown beyond a local uprising.

In the meantime, Emir Feisal had to receive representatives from the tribes in the north and persuade them to put aside their traditional feuds to join in the Arab Revolt. Lawrence had the unenviable task of serving two masters—Allenby and Feisal. He had to decide what to reveal or hold back to each master. He could not reveal the entire British plan to Feisal for security reasons. He could not be over optimistic of Arab capabilities to Allenby. Yet Feisal trusted him and relied upon him to deliver the British promises. Allenby needed his advice on the Arab situation and to lead the Arabs when the time came.

In October 1917, Lawrence was told that Allenby planned to launch an offensive to capture Jaffa and Jerusalem. After some discussion, Lawrence decided that the Arab inland rebellion should wait. But they could not remain inactive. Lawrence led a raid to blow up one of the three railway bridges at the Yarmuk Valley from 5-8 November 1917. During the expedition, one of the Arabs, Abdul el Kader, deserted and it was correctly assumed that he was a Turkish spy. After things went wrong, they only managed to blow up part of the railway line near Deraa.

In late November, Lawrence went with a local sheikh to explore Deraa. They were disguised as local peasants. However, the spy who had earlier deserted informed Hajim Bey, the governor of Deraa, whose men arrested Lawrence. The governor was a homosexual who had his guards flog Lawrence before sexually assaulting him. During the night, Lawrence escaped with the assistance of an Arab sympathiser. Although he would eventually recover physically, his emotional scars would never be healed.

Lawrence returned to Allenby's GHQ in time to participate in the capture of Jerusalem. He was allowed to enter the city as part of Allenby's staff. For someone who graduated in history and was familiar with the Crusades, "it was the supreme moment of the war."

THE MAKING OF "LAWRENCE OF ARABIA"

In February 1918, an American journalist, Lowell Thomas arrived at Akaba with some cameramen. Their assignment was to search for material to might appeal to the Americans to support the war. Lawrence realized that the publicity might help the Arab cause and arranged for meetings with Feisal and other Arab leaders.

In September 1918, Allenby's army attacked the Turks in Palestine. The Arabs cut the railway lines around Deraa and the Turks abandoned Damascus by 30 September. Allenby allowed only the Arab forces and Lawrence to enter the city. It was the crowning achievement for Lawrence. The tide of victory would sweep even further north to Aleppo.

But Lawrence did not tarry long. Instead, he sought permission to leave for England. In October, he pleaded for Arab self-rule in Syria. But the French were keen to continue their rule over Syria after the war. The British government did not want to antagonise a former war-time ally.

The post war agreements resulted in the British being given mandates over Palestine and Iraq. The French were allowed to retain their colony of Syria. Lawrence was tormented, feeling that he had betrayed Emir Feisal and the Arabs after all they had sacrificed. It was not until 1936 that the French allowed the Arabs to govern Syria.

In August 1919, the American journalist Lowell Thomas released his documentary about Lawrence and Allenby's roles in the capture of Jerusalem. It was an instant hit with the public who were satiated by the horrors of trench warfare during the war. Lawrence had become a romantic and popular figure in the public imagination.

In early 1919, he began to write *"The Seven Pillars of Wisdom"* which was a record of his wartime experiences during the Arab Revolt. He had nearly completed the manuscript and lent some copies to friends for comment. In November 1919, he lost the first draft of his book while changing trains at Reading station. His friends persuaded him to rewrite the book which was a slow and painful process. By early May 1920, he had written "only about 400,000 words."

He bought some land at Pole Hill, near Epping Forest with the intention of starting a printing press. He made a large financial gift to Janet Laurie's family whose mother was seriously ill. He had apparently overlooked the fact that she had previously rejected his proposal of marriage.

In January 1921, he joined the Colonial Office as adviser to Winston Churchill. By March 1921, the Middle East settlement was reached. The costs of the continued Iraq rebellion caused the British to rethink their strategy. They granted autonomy to Iraq under Emir Feisal. Emir Abdullah was allowed to rule Trans-Jordan. Eventually, the Hedjaz was absorbed into modern day Saudi Arabia. For Lawrence, the agreement had come three years too late.

Lawrence tried to publish an abridged version of his *"Seven Pillars of Wisdom"* by condensing some specimen chapters. But he was not well known in America and the sales were poor. The project stalled. Instead of abridgement, by September that year he decided to work on an expanded version that far exceeded the original lost version. He eventually commissioned some 41 illustrations from 11 artists for his work which substantially increased its cost.

WHEN FAME BECAME A BURDEN

By 1922, he became depressed as a reaction to his wartime exertions. In desperation, he applied to join the RAF in August 1922 under the name of John Hume Ross. He was then aged 34, had become famous and had some income from his books. Why did he choose to enlist in the ranks of the RAF? He did not find public office or an academic career appealing. If he served in the ranks, the duties were not taxing and he had the time to write. Between August 1922 and May 1935, he arranged for a subscription edition to his *"Seven Pillars"*. He also worked on a translation of Homer's *"Odyssey."* He was a prolific letter writer; some 6,000 letters written during this period have survived.

In December 1922, the press learnt about his posting to RAF Farnborough. In January 1923, he declined the offer of a commission by Trenchard and was dismissed from the RAF to avoid further embarrassment.

In May 1923, he joined the Tank Corps as TE Shaw. He was extremely unhappy in the Tank Corps and his mental stability was further unhinged. His friends were alarmed and persuaded him to work on a subscription edition of the *"Seven Pillars."* However, the price would be exorbitant and Lawrence did not want the public to think that he was greedy. So he declared that he would forego his share of the profit from the sales of the subscription edition.

But the revision and the printing process took longer than he expected. He commissioned even more illustrations from the leading artists of the day. He insisted on minor printing changes such as every page should commence with a new paragraph. The result was that costs soared way above his budget and his bank refused further credit. He had to auction his land at Pole Hill. Finally, he agreed to let Jonathan Cape publish an abridged edition. But he could not gain financially from it since he had earlier renounced his share of the profits. The abridged version was published as *"Revolt in the Desert."*

He became even more depressed and threatened to commit suicide if he was not allowed to re-join the RAF. The government was alarmed by the potential scandal and agreed to let him re-enlist at RAF Cranwell. At his request, he was posted overseas to RAF Karachi.

By late 1928, the press began to speculate that he was engaged in spying activities in Afghanistan. He was shipped back but when he arrived at Plymouth, the press was waiting for him. He was eventually posted to RAF Cattewater, near the seaplane base at Plymouth. Here at least the commanding officer was Sydney Smith who had known Lawrence since the Cairo days. Lawrence worked in the marine workshop section.

In February 1932, Lawrence was part of a team in the Marine Craft Section (MCS) that tested and helped to develop small high speed launches that were designed to pick up downed airmen from the sea. Most of these launches were designed by the British Power Boat Company (BPC) and Vosper Thorneycroft.

The Marine Craft Section (MCS) of the RAF had been formed in April 1918. It eventually became the RAF Air Sea Rescue Service in February 1941. By the end of the Second World War, the Service had rescued an estimated 13,000 downed aircrew.

His friends wanted to donate a motor cycle to him but he refused to accept and paid for it himself. As he wanted only the best motor cycles, he bought an expensive Brough Superiors model.

In February 1935, he retired from the RAF at the age of 46. When he retired to his cottage at Cloud Hills, Dorset, he found no peace to write as journalists besieged him. On 13 May 1935, he was riding his motor bike when he tried to avoid two boys on bicycles. He crashed and suffered brain damage. On 19 May, he succumbed to his injuries and died.

HIS CHARACTER ANALSYED

Thomas Edward Lawrence was born on a 已Yin Earth未Goat day in the 申Monkey month. The申Monkey month represented early autumn when metal was the strongest element. There is a good deal of metal in his chart. There is 辛Yin Metal in his 酉Rooster hour. There is also 庚Yang Metal in the Heavenly Stem above his申 Monkey month. Too much metal exhausts the earth.

Thomas Edward Lawrence 16-8-1888

时Hour	日Day			月Month			年Year
癸 Yin Water	已 Yin Earth			庚 Yang Metal			戊 Yang Earth
酉 Rooster	未 Goat			申 Monkey			子 Rat
辛 Yin Metal	已 Yin Earth	丁 Yin Fire	乙 Yin Wood	庚 Yang Metal	壬 Yang Water	戊 Yang Earth	癸 Yin Water

The fire element is needed to produce the earth. There is some 丁Yin Fire in his 未Goat day of birth. But this fire is too weak to produce earth. He was born in the autumn season when fire was weak. There was also the 癸Yin Water in the Heavenly Stem above his 酉Rooster hour. There is some more癸Yin Water inside his 子 Rat year of birth. This meant that his fire is surrounded by metal and water. This structure weakened his fire even further.

Since he was born on an earth day master, he could have been reserved and withdrawn. One of the characteristics of earth is to be secretive, to cover up like the planet earth covering up the metals hidden inside. But he was also known to be talkative and not shy at all. He had to be somewhat outgoing, otherwise he would not have been able to socialise and communicate with the Arabs. How do we account for this discrepancy?

There was too much metal in his chart. Generally speaking, metal people liked to talk, just as the bell or wind musical instrument is designed to make a sound. However, he was not a publicity hound. Certainly, he did not crave attention. He preferred to be left alone to continue his pursuits. Therein lay the horns of his dilemma. He needed publicity to plead the cause of self-governance for the Arabs. When his task was done, he asked for nothing more than privacy. Unfortunately for him, the media did not forget him so easily.

HIS ACHIEVEMENTS

The 乙Yin Wood in his 未Goat day of birth represented his authority, fame or power. In the context of the events that occurred in his life, this乙Yin Wood will become very important to him. The 乙Yin Wood is weak because he was born in the autumn season when metal was strong. However, at least he has this authority star even though it was weak. The presence of this star and the weak condition of this same authority star would help to explain the events that occurred in his life. If he did not have this authority star, he would not have been able to persuade the Arabs to join him to fight the Turks in Syria. But when he joined the RAF and the Tank Corps, he enlisted as a private.

The elements that he needed were 丙Yang Fire and 癸Yin Water. He only had the癸Yin Water in his chart. He needed the 丙 Yang Fire which represented sunlight to warm his chart. When he encountered the 丙Yang Fire in his luck cycle or annual pillars, then he will have better potential for achievement.

Thomas Edward Lawrence Luck Cycle

37	27	17	7
甲 Yang Wood	癸 Yin Water	壬 Yang Water	辛 Yin Metal
子 Rat	亥 Pig	戌 Dog	酉 Rooster
癸 Yin Water	壬 甲 Yang Yang Water Wood	戊 辛 丁 Yang Yin Yin Earth Metal Fire	辛 Yin Metal

77	67	57	47
戊 Yang Earth	丁 Yin Fire	丙 Yang Fire	乙 Yin Wood
巳 Snake	卯 Rabbit	寅 Tiger	丑 Ox
丙 戊 庚 Yang Yang Yang Fire Earth Metal	乙 Yin Wood	甲 丙 戊 Yang Yang Yang Wood Fire Earth	己 癸 辛 Yin Yin Yin Earth Water Metal

He joined Military Intelligence in December 1914, which was the year of 甲Yang Wood 寅Tiger. The fire is in the growth stage in the寅Tiger year. In December 1916, he began to win the trust of Emir Feisal. This was the year of 丙Yang Fire 辰Dragon. The丙 Yang Fire that he needed was present in the Heavenly Stem of the year.

In 1917, he led the Arabs to cut the railway line and attack Akaba from the inland approaches. The year 1917 was the year of 丁Yin Fire 巳Snake. The 巳Snake year represented early summer when fire was the strongest element. There is丙Yang Fire in the巳Snake year. There was also丁Yin Fire in the Heavenly Stem above the Snake. This structure made the fire very strong in 1917 and helped him to achieve his military victories.

But if this was such a good year for him, why was he captured and sexually abused in late November of the same year? Partly it was his own fault for making his way in enemy territory. The other reason was that he was betrayed by someone he already distrusted. The November month was the 辛Yin Metal 亥Pig month. The亥 Pig month clashed with the巳Snake year. This clash indicated that he should have been more careful during this month. Instead, he made mistakes that brought about his capture. However, since the fire was strong during this year, his captivity would not last long. He escaped during the night.

In 1919, the year of 己Yin Earth 未Goat, he began writing the book that would make him even more famous, *"The Seven Pillars of Wisdom."* He was relieved that the Middle East settlement was reached in March 1921. But it came three years too late and had probably soured the relationships between the Arabs and the British.

HIS PROBLEMS

In 1922, he joined the RAF under a false name. This was the year of壬Yang Water 戌Dog. The戌Dog represented autumn season when metal was strong. There was壬Yang Water in the Heavenly Stem above the戌Dog year. The fire that he needed was no longer available. His difficulties were about to begin.

The press publicity that dogged him caused him to leave the RAF. In March 1923, he joined the Tank Corps, also under a false identity. The year 1923 was the year of 癸Yin Water 亥Pig. The 亥Pig represented the winter season when water was strong. There was also癸Yin Water in the Heavenly Stem above the亥Pig. This structure only made the water even stronger. The fire that he needed was extinguished.

Furthermore, the亥Pig had a Three Harmony relationship with his 未Goat day master that resulted in wood. The wood element represented his fame. It was his fame that would the source of his problems in the years to come.

In December 1923, he published the subscription version of his *"Seven Pillars of Wisdom."* However, he had agreed to forego his share of the profits. So he did not make any money from the venture.

In August 1925, he told his friends that he wanted to commit suicide. The British government was alarmed at the possible scandal that his suicide might cause. Trenchard agreed to let him re-join the RAF, again under a false name. The year 1925 was the year of 乙Yin Wood 丑Ox. The 丑Ox represented winter when water was strong. There was no fire available for him during this year. His problems would continue to hound him. In December 1928, he had to return from his posting in Afghanistan.

In February 1932, he was part of a team that worked on the testing and development of high speed launches for the RAF. This was the year of 壬Yang Water 申Monkey. The申Monkey year had a Three Harmony relationship with his 子Rat luck cycle which resulted in the water element. Water represented his wealth. But his birth chart already showed that too much water was present. So he would not become wealthy during this period. Instead, he had to wrestle with money problems.

In February 1935, he retired from the RAF. This was the year of 乙Yin Wood 亥Pig. The亥Pig year represented the winter season when water was strong. His financial problems would only get worse.

THE DEEPER ISSUES

But it was not just a matter of trying to avoid the media publicity. His deeper issues were more wide ranging. He could not have any satisfactory relationship with the opposite sex. Although he came from a well to do family, he faced constant money problems. He wanted to stay in the military services both for the income and the adventure. But he also yearned to be remembered as a writer, not as an adventurer. Despite his fame, he felt depressed and even contemplated suicide. He seemed incapable of ever finding happiness.

He was a weak 己Yin Earth day master born in the autumn season when metal was strong. The metal was so strong in his chart that it exhausted his earth. His 申Monkey month of birth had a combination relationship with his 子Rat year of birth that resulted in the water element. In theory, earth controlled water. But too much water threatened to wash away the earth, which was already weakened by the excessive metal. This structure meant that while he was a creative and imaginative person, he felt insecure and lonely. The overly strong water made him too emotional and prone to depressions.

The water element represented his wealth and his women. Too much water did not necessarily mean more money and more female companionship. Instead, it indicated that he could not control his money or his relationships with his female friends. The ordeal of his sexual abuse in the desert left deep psychological scars on him that refused to heal. Inevitably, this traumatic experience would mar his relationships with women for the rest of his life.

He wanted to be remembered for his literary works rather than for his military victories. It did not quite work out that way. To the public, he was the "Lawrence of Arabia" as shown bigger than life on the screen in the 1962 David Lean production with Peter O'Toole and Omar Sharif in the lead roles. It was likely that only some of the movie going public was aware that he wrote *"Seven Pillars of Wisdom"*—and perhaps even fewer still had read it.

CHAPTER SEVEN

HISTORY AT THE CROSSROADS: HO CHI MINH AND THE STRUGGLE FOR FREEDOM

"Tell the Americans . . . . the Vietnamese would never fight the Americans."
(Ho Chi Minh to Major Archimedes Patti, circa September 1945)

THE FOURTH CROSSROADS IN HISTORY: MAY-OCTOBER 1954

On 9 October 1954, soldiers of the French *Corps expeditionnaire* crossed the Paul Doumer Bridge that laid across the Red River in Hanoi. The troops embarked on troopships bound for another French colony where another war of independence had broken out—Algeria. The French had been defeated at Dien Bien Phu in May 1954. The city of Hanoi was handed over to Vo Nguyen Giap's regiments.

It marked the end of French rule in Indo China. The Geneva Agreements on 7 May 1954 provided for elections to be held in North and South Vietnam. The country was temporarily divided along the 16th Parallel. But what was supposed to be a temporary division would last for the next 21 years.

However, the Eisenhower Administration refused to recognise the provisions of the Geneva Agreements. They had been alarmed by the ferocity of the fighting in the Korean War which had just ended on 27 July 1953 by an armistice. At that time, the Cold War was at its height and the American governments of the day were haunted by the spectre of Communism spreading its tentacles. They concluded that they had to make a stand somewhere to confront the spread of Communism. What better place to do so than an obscure, far away country known as Vietnam? Without any official declaration of war by either side, the Vietnam War would soon begin.

Unfortunately for them, one frail old man stood in the way. He would direct the tiger to maul the elephant—as he had previously mauled the French. His name was Ho Chi Minh. Both sides had just crossed the fourth crossroads in history.

PART I: THE MAN AND HIS TIMES 1890-1945

THE EARLY YEARS OF HO CHI MINH

When he was born on 19 May 1890 in Hoang Tru village, he was given the name Nguyen Sinh Sac. Later he would be known by many names such as Nguyen Sinh Voung, Nguyen Tat Tanh ("he who will succeed") and Nguyen Ai Quoc. His father was Nguyen Sinh Cong and his mother was Hoang Thi Loan. He was the youngest of three children. He had a sister, Nguyen Thi Tanh, born in 1884 and a brother, Nguyen Sinh Khiem, born in 1888.

His father was a Confucian scholar who passed the examination at the second attempt. He could have lived a comfortable life as a government official. Instead, he chose to live the life of a simple peasant. He was imbibed with the rebel spirit. The Nghe An province had long been a hotbed for rebellions against the Chinese rulers.

In August 1900, Ho's father was summoned to work as a clerk for the imperial examinations at Thanh Hoa, about 500 km from Hue. He had taken his elder son, Khiem, with him. Ho was left behind with his mother. His father decided to stop at the village of Kim Lien on the way back in order to build a tomb for his parents. While they were away, Ho's mother delivered her fourth child, a boy named Nguyen Sinh Xin. But the delivery weakened her further and she died on 10 February 1901. Ho had to go round from house to house to ask for milk. It was a sobering experience for a ten year old boy. Upon hearing the news of his wife's death, his father hurriedly returned and took the family back to Hoang Tru village.

THE ODYSSEY OF HO CHI MINH 1911-1944

In 1911, he left Saigon on a ship bound for France. It was the beginning of his Odyssey which would last some three decades. He would not return to Indo-China until 1944.

He was then only 21 years old and unsure of himself. He only had a vague idea that he wanted freedom for his countrymen. He also visited the US briefly but apparently it made no impression on him. His travels would give him a cosmopolitan view of world affairs. He also learnt to speak some English and French. He worked at whatever jobs he could find to support himself, including work as cook, gardener and laundryman.

He saw first-hand how the poor lived in the country of his colonial masters. He realised that the French treated their poor folk no better than the way they treated the natives in their far flung colonies. He seemed bemused that the cry of the French Revolution—*"Liberte, Egalite, Fraternite"* (Liberty, Equality, Fraternity)—did not seem to apply in modern day France.

He joined the French Socialist Party in 1919. When that party broke up in 1920, he helped to form the Comintern Party in Paris. In July 1921, he broke up with his friends in Paris. This left him stranded with little money to get by.

On 22 June 1922, he was detained and brought to meet Albert Sarraut, the French Minister of Colonies. Sarraut alternately threatened him and bribed him to no avail. He told Sarraut that what he wanted was "freedom for his countrymen, nothing less and nothing more." In June 1923, he went to Russia.

In 1924, he returned to China. He recruited Vietnamese exiles to join the Communist Youth League of Vietnam. Sometime in 1927, he left his Chinese wife, Tuyet Minh. In 1930, he founded the Vietnam Communist Party with Russian assistance.

In May 1931, he had an affair with Minh Khai. But she left him and married Le Hong Phong in July 1935. She was arrested in Saigon in November 1940 for subversive activities and sentenced to death.

On 6 June 1931, Ho was arrested in Hong Kong but was released on 28 December 1932. On 6 January 1933, he was again arrested in Singapore. But the British were eager to release him on 22 January 1933. He was deported to Xiamen or Amoy. By 1938, he had returned to China. He founded the Vietminh Front with Vo Nguyen Giap in 1941. In 1944, he returned to Tonkin.

THE FIRST CROSSROADS IN HISTORY: JULY 1945

Major Archimedes Patti was sent by the Office of Strategic Service (OSS) to Indo-China in June 1944. He recalled that he met Ho on 30 April 1945. He was struck by Ho's intelligence and determination to cling to his vision of winning independence for his country. Ho used his network to rescue downed US airmen and help them escape to southern China.

In May 1945, Patti met Jean Sainteny who was a veteran of the *Deuxieme Bureau,* the French version of the OSS. Sainteny had been sent to organise an operation called Mission 5 or M-5. The French had the intelligence network along the Indo-China border. But the loss of the military garrison to the Japanese during the war was a serious setback. The French needed American help to provide weapons and communications. Major Patti turned Sainteny down.

Sainteny also found Ho to be intelligent and determined about his quest for independence for his country.

By early March 1945 when the defeat of Germany seemed inevitable, the Japanese disarmed the French garrisons in Indo-China and made the troops prisoners. Those who resisted were killed. However, three battalions of the 5th Infantry Regiment marched for 51 days through the Thai highlands until they reached southern China. For the first time, the Vietminh was presented with a power vacuum. The Japanese installed the emperor Bao Dai as a puppet ruler. But the Japanese, the emperor and the sectarian sects were no match for the well-organized communist and Vietminh cells.

In July 1945, Ho was sick with malaria and dysentery. Major Archimedes Patti recalled that the OSS treated Ho with quinine and sulfa which helped him to recover. However, Vo Nguyen Giap disputed this version of events. He said that an elderly man from a nearby village was summoned and he treated Ho until he recovered. Whoever it was that saved Ho Chi Minh's life, the first crossroads in history had been crossed.

President Roosevelt was opposed to colonialism but he eventually got tired of arguing about it with Winston Churchill. When pressed for a statement on US policy in Indo-China, he replied "I don't want to hear any more about Indo-China." President Roosevelt died on 12 April 1945 before the end of the Second World War.

From May to August 1945, two OSS teams led by Major Archimedes Patti and Allison Thomas trained Vietminh guerrillas to raid Japanese outposts. When the news of the Japanese surrender in August spread, the Japanese handed power to Bao Dai and left the country. For the second time, the Vietminh was presented with a power vacuum.

Major Archimedes Patti later recorded his impressions of the meeting with Ho Chi Minh in *"Why Vietnam? Prelude to America's Albatross"* (University of California Press, 1980).

THE SECOND CROSSROADS IN HISTORY: SEPTEMBER 1945

After the defeat of the Japanese in August 1945, Ho proclaimed the Democratic Republic of Vietnam on 2 September 1945. He became both president and prime minister until 1955. He was careful to send feelers to both the US and China asking them to recognise his country. China gave recognition to the new republic of Vietnam. Ho Chi Minh even quoted from the American Declaration of Independence. As if that was not enough, he told the Americans that they had promised a date when independence would be given to the Philippines. The Americans had kept their word. Why could they not do the same for Vietnam?

Initially, the Truman Administration was receptive as it followed President Roosevelt's policy of opposing colonialism. At that time, the Cold War had not yet started. Later President Truman balked at antagonising the French who were, after all, former wartime allies. The Americans allowed the French to reoccupy their former possessions. The second crossroads in history had been crossed by the Truman Administration.

PART II: THE LOST CAUSE

THE "*CORPS EXPEDITIONNAIRE*" VERSUS "THE PEOPLE'S ARMY"

From 1946 to 1951, the French fought an indecisive war with the Vietminh in Indo-China. The French had to supply their far flung garrisons by supplies travelling along *Route Coloniale 4* (RC 4). As the route passed through mountainous and wooded terrain, it was ideal for ambushes by the Vietminh. By 1950, the civil war in China had ended with the defeat of Chiang Kai-Shek. The Chinese Red Army was freed to provide troops and supplies to the Vietminh. In mid-September 1950, General Vo Nyugen Giap attacked and drove the French away from RC 4. In a campaign that lasted about two months, he inflicted about 6,000 French casualties. The French command panicked and wanted to evacuate the frontier garrisons.

General Jean de Lattre de Tassigny had a son, Lt. Bernard who was serving with the *1er Chasseurs a Cheval* regiment in the Red River Delta. He was probably moved by his son's letters which appealed to him to rescue the *Corps expeditionnaire* whose leaders began to exhibit a defeatist attitude. When General de Lattre was offered command by the French government, he demanded and obtained the civil powers of High Commissioner as well as military Commander-in-Chief.

Upon disembarkation at Saigon, his first act was to dismiss the commander of the Saigon garrison when he found the guard of honour to be unsatisfactory.

Then he cancelled the orders to evacuate all women and children from Hanoi. He rescinded all preparations made to withdraw the troops south of the 17th Parallel. He dismissed many officers and sent them back to France. They were replaced by other officers who were willing to fight.

His chance to fight came when General Vo Nguyen Giap tried to infiltrate into the Red River Delta and fought the French army in three battles from January to June 1951. As these battles were fought in the open, the French could use their advantages of modern firepower and airpower. This time it was the Vietminh who suffered about 9,000 casualties.

These half victories allowed the French to occupy Hanoi and the Red River Delta. But General de Lattre paid a personal price for his success. On the night of 29-30 May 1951, his son, Lt. Bernard was killed during the defence of a hill near Ninh Binh against Giap's Regiment 88. The General accompanied his son's body back to Paris for burial. But his son's death broke his spirit and when he returned to Indo-China, he had no heart to continue the fight. By the time he died from cancer in January 1952, he was already an embittered man.

THE DAWN OF DEFEAT: THE BATTLE OF NA SAN (NOVEMBER-DECMBER 1952)

The French had established a chain of tiny outposts, lightly garrisoned between the Red and Black Rivers in North West Tonkin in 1952. The purpose was to block or hamper the movement of large scale enemy formations and to lure them into attacking the strongest garrisons. By mid-October 1952, the Vietminh had overrun all the outposts and the French withdrew to Na San behind the Black River.

The little known Battle of Na San was fought from 23 November 1952 until 2 December 1952. The main battle was fought during the night of 23-24 November 1952 at the outpost known as PA8. This dug-out was held by 110 men of the 11th Company, III Battalion, 5th Infantry Regiment under Captain Letestu. Without any preparatory fire, at about 8.00 pm a Vietminh battalion attacked and took the defenders by surprise. After a desperate hand-to-hand struggle, the defenders drove off the Vietminh by about 9.30 pm at a cost of 15 men killed and another 15 injured. The Vietminh casualties were not known.

Both sides learnt different lessons from the same battle. General Vo Ngyuen Giap realized that he had to take the higher ground both for observation and supporting artillery fire. He had to plan for a prolonged battle rather than incur heavy casualties by using "human waves" attacks. This in turn meant that he had to prepare for adequate logistics to provide food and ammunition for a longer period.

The French believed that it was possible to establish a garrison of troops in the remote upper regions of the Red River Delta. As these garrisons would be supplied and reinforced from the air, the concept was known as *"base aero-terrestre"* (air bridge).

The valley of Dien Bien Phu in Tonkin lay close to the Laos border. If this village was occupied and supported by air, the French could send patrols to harass the enemy using the Ho Chi Minh trail. It was also hoped that this garrison would lure the enemy into a decisive battle that could end the war. The Geneva conference was scheduled for 20-21 July 1954 and each side needed a convincing military victory that they could bring to the bargaining table.

By mid-1953, the new Commander-in-Chief, General Henri Navarre decided to occupy Dien Bien Phu. On 20 November 1953, six battalions of paratroops seized Dien Bien Phu from the Vietminh in *Operation Castor*.

TWILIGHT OF AN EMPIRE: THE BATTLE OF DIEN BIEN PHU (MARCH-MAY 1954)

The French constructed a series of forts, the northernmost being Gabrielle and Beatrice to the northeast. The garrisons that surrounded the airfield in the centre were Anne-Marie, Huguette, Dominique, Claudine and Elaine. The southernmost garrison was Isabelle which had its own airfield. Dien Bien Phu was eleven miles long and three miles at its widest point.

The chief engineer, Major Andre Sudrat estimated that he needed about 30,000 tons of construction material to build the two airstrips at Dien Bien Phu. The *Armee de L'Air* had only about 80 transport aircraft, mostly C-47 Dakotas and some Fairchild C-119A Packets. They could only deliver about 150 tons per day, most of which had to be the more important food and ammunition. The supply battle with the enemy had already been lost before it even began.

The bases at Dien Bien Phu were surrounded by highlands that were covered by dense vegetation. Even if the enemy could position their artillery on the slopes of the mountains overlooking the bases, Colonel Charles Piroth, the senior artillery officer, believed that "they could not fire three rounds before our guns could locate them." His main artillery consisted of 24 howitzers of 105mm calibre and 4 howitzers of 155mm calibre. He was also given three heavy mortar companies and 4 quad fifties which were four barrelled anti-aircraft machine guns, deadly when used against attacking human waves of infantry. But howitzers were designed to fire at an angle, just like mortars and to fire in all directions. This meant that the gunners were exposed and could not fire from protective casemates. The lack of overhead protection for the gun pits would be sorely missed by the gunners during the imminent battle.

But there were several ominous differences from Na San. Na San had occupied about half the size of Dien Bien Phu. Although both garrisons were held by about the same number of battalions, this meant that Na San was both easier to defend and more heavily defended. The airstrip at Na San had been surrounded by the cluster of hills which were occupied by the defenders. Besides the strongpoints in the hills, there was a second ring of defence which blocked the attackers from infiltrating between the hills to isolate individual defensive positions. The enemy could not overlook Na San from any high ground. Instead, the ground in front of the defenders was level or sloped away.

At Dien Bien Phu, the defenders occupied the valley instead of the high ground. They cleared the jungle for several hundred metres around their strong points to give them an unobstructed view of any attacking enemy. But this had the reverse effect of giving their enemy in the hills a clear view of the French positions.

From late December 1953, the Vietminh began to observe and map the defending units at Dien Bien Phu. General Vo Nguyen Giap assembled two armies—one army of about 20,000 porters to carry the supplies of food on bicycles or on their backs and another fighting army of four divisions, perhaps 50,000 men. In order to supply one kilo of rice for the fighting man, the porter required ten kilos of rice for himself. The artillery was dragged up the mountains piece by piece. The Vietminh eventually assembled 48 105 mm howitzers, 48 75 mm guns, 48 120mm mortars and 75 mm recoilless rifles and 36 anti-aircraft guns.

The artillery was hidden in caves on the reverse slopes of the mountains. When the guns fired, the French could not even see their positions, let alone bring down ringing fire. But the risk was that if the trajectories were wrongly calculated, the guns could not change their positions.

Dien Bien Phu was held by seven parachute battalions and eleven infantry battalions under the command of General Rene Cogny. Some of the officers who would play prominent roles in the forthcoming battle were Colonel Christian de Castries, Lt.-Colonel Pierre "Gars Pierre" Langlais and Major Marcel "Bruno" Bigeard.

The Vietminh units involved in the struggle were Divisions 304, 308, 312 and 316. They were supported by artillery from Heavy Division 351 and Independent Infantry Regiment 148.

At about 3.00 pm on 13 March 1954, the first salvos of the Vietminh artillery pounded the air strip at Anne-Marie. Three Grumman F8F Bearcat fighters immediately took off. The remaining eight were destroyed in their sandbagged pens. The Vietminh infantry began to assault the garrisons at Anne-Marie, Beatrice and Gabrielle.

Colonel Piroth was shocked that the enemy could bring up guns the size of 105 mm calibre. He realized too late that his gunners could not locate the positions of the enemy guns. Instead of howitzers, he required guns that could fire a flat trajectory. The only such guns available were the 75mm guns mounted on each of the ten M24 Chafee tanks. However, to get the tanks in position was cumbersome and time consuming. Three of the tanks had been deployed at the southernmost outpost at Isabelle. In any case, all the tanks were eventually knocked out by the enemy artillery. At one stroke, the French lost their advantages of armour and air support.

THE THIRD CROSSROADS IN HISTORY: MAY 1954

The French government appealed to the Americans for help. The Americans considered sending in their Boeing B-29 Superfortress heavy bombers to bomb the enemy positions. But they were wary about provoking China and the Soviet Union into a wider conflict. The Americans had just extricated their army from the Korean War in November 1953 by means of a negotiated truce. Unwittingly, their decision had made them cross the third crossroads in history.

At about 5.30 pm on 7 May, the Vietminh broke into the headquarters bunkers and took General Rene Cogny and his staff prisoners. Around 8.00 pm on 7 May, Colonel Lalande led the remnants of several companies to try a break out from Isabelle. The effort made little progress in the darkness as they could not tell friend from foe. By 1.50 am, Colonel Lalande had sent his last radio message before surrendering.

On 4 June 1954, General Henri Navarre was relieved of his command. Michael Maclear was a journalist who also made a television documentary of the Vietnam War. In his book, *"Vietnam: The Ten Thousand Day War"* (Thames Methuen, 1981) he quoted General Navarre as saying that he "accepted responsibility but not any guilt" for Dien Bien Phu.

John Keegan was a consultant editor in the mid-1970s to the multi volume *"Ballantine's Illustrated History of the Violent Century."* He also contributed several books to the series, one of which was *"Dien Bien Phu"* (Random House, 1974). He argued that despite the unfavourable terrain, it might still have been possible for the French to win at Dien Bien Phu if they had planned it differently. In the event, Dien Bien Phu turned out to be a repetition of the artillery duels of Verdun and the tunnel warfare of Vauban, both of which were battles of the First World War.

While the battle of Dien Bien Phu was being fought, there were other simultaneous battles throughout Tonkin. The French *Armee de L'Air* was hard pressed to supply other air bases at Pleiku, Seno and Xien Khouang. In a similar way, while Khe Sanh was besieged from January to April 1968, the bigger campaign was the Tet Offensive from January to late February 1968. But the loss of Dien Bien Phu would signal the end of French rule in Indo China even if the other battles could be won.

Later John Keegan would establish his reputation as a military historian with the publication of such works as *"The Face of Battle"* (Jonathan Cape, 1976) and *"The Mask of Command"* (Penguin, 1987).

Martin Windrow admitted that he was not trained academically as a historian. This apparent "deficiency" has not deterred him from writing the definitive history of Dien Bien Phu, *"The Last Valley: Dien Bien Phu and the French defeat in Vietnam"* (Cassell Military Series, 2005). The French army had suffered its worst defeat since Dunkirk in May 1940.

The definitive biography about Ho Chi Minh still remains Professor William Duiker's *"Ho Chi Minh"* (Hyperion, 2000).

PART III: AN ANALYSIS OF THE MAN

HIS CHARACTER

Ho Chi Minh was born on a 庚 Yang Metal 子 Rat day in the 巳 Snake month. The 巳 Snake month represented early summer. Fire is the strongest element in summer. His metal is said to be weak in summer. But the metal had roots in the 巳 Snake month.

Ho Chi Minh 19-5-1890

时 Hour	日 Day	月 Month			年 Year		
巳 Yin Earth	庚 Yang Metal	辛 Yin Metal			庚 Yang Metal		
卯 Rabbit	子 Rat	巳 Snake			寅 Tiger		
乙 Yin Wood	癸 Yin Water	丙 Yang Fire	戊 Yang Earth	庚 Yang Metal	甲 Yang Wood	丙 Yang Fire	戊 Yang Earth

The 巳 Snake belonged to the metal frame together with the 酉 Rooster and the 丑 Ox. This 巳 Snake month would be vital to him. The 巳 Snake provided him the roots for his metal day and the metal in the Heavenly Stem above his 寅 Tiger year.

This structure indicated that he could endure hardship, was stubborn, passionate about his dreams or ideals. The 巳 Snake month represented summer when fire is the strongest element. Fire represented his authority.

His authority star is represented by 丙 Yang Fire. There is 丙 Yang Fire in his 巳 Snake month and his 寅 Tiger year. This indicated that he has power or authority. The fire also gave him the passion to pursue his aim of achieving independence for his country.

He had many 庚Yang Metal Friends. These Friends were influential and could assist him. However, the same Friends star could also represent competitors such as war time enemies. His enemies might be powerful military nations such as Japan, France and the US.

The 庚Yang Metal day master shows that he has a stubborn and unyielding character. He can also endure hardship. The庚Yang Metal represented hard metal such as a telephone post or lamppost. This metal needed to be forged in order to be useful. When fire forged metal, the metal person will have to suffer hardship. The fire in the巳Snake gave him the passion to pursue his dreams unwaveringly.

If he could not endure hardship, he would not have been able to survive living on basic necessities in the jungles.

He badly needed the 壬Yang Water to cool down the heat in his chart. In addition, he also needed the elements of 戊Yang Earth, 丙Yang Fire and 丁Yin Fire. The戊Yang Earth and丙Yang Fire were already available in his 巳Snake day and 寅Tiger year of birth. Therefore, he only needed the壬Yang Water and the丁Yin Fire. When these elements were encountered in his luck cycles, his prospects of success would improve.

The壬Yang Water arrived when he was in his 申Monkey luck cycle when he was aged 26 in 1916. If that was the case, why could he not achieve what he wanted during this period? The壬Yang Water was not in season during the申Monkey luck cycle. The申Monkey represented autumn when metal was the strongest element. The申Monkey also had an ungrateful punishment relationship with his巳Snake month.

His wealth and women star is represented by wood. The wood element is weak in summer. There is wood only in his 寅Tiger year and 卯Rabbit hour. These pillars are not his marriage pillar which should be his day earthly branch. He was not that interested in women. There seemed to be some evidence that he considered women a distraction to the Cause. If he had the opportunity to have affairs with women, he would do so. Otherwise, he did not care to pursue women. Instead, he was more devoted to pursuing independence from foreign domination for his country.

Some sources said that he had children. If so, he apparently did not maintain contact with them. His 子Rat day master had an uncivilized punishment relationship with his 卯Rabbit hour. As the hour of birth indicated the children's pillar, this indicated that his relationship with his children was not harmonious.

He was pragmatic. The plentiful presence of 庚Yang Metal in his chart indicated that he had many Friends who could assist him. These Friends could be the US after the Second World War or China and the Soviet Union. He would turn to whoever was willing to assist him, irrespective of whether they were democracies or communists. If the US had helped him, it was probable that he would not have turned to the Communist powers.

HIS STRUGGLES

In 1913, he became the co-founder of the Comintern Party in Paris at the age of only 23. This was the year of 癸Yin Water 丑 Ox. He was then relatively inexperienced at the age of 23 and in his luck cycle of 癸Yin Water 未Goat. His未Goat luck cycle clashed with the丑Ox year. He was not likely to rise to power during this period.

Ho Chi Minh Luck Cycle

36	26			16			6	
乙 Yin Wood	甲 Yang Wood			癸 Yin Water			壬 Yang Water	
酉 Rooster	申 Monkey			未 Goat			午 Horse	
辛 Yin Metal	庚 Yang Metal	壬 Yang Water	戊 Yang Earth	已 Yin Earth	丁 Yin Fire	乙 Yin Wood	丁 Yin Fire	已 Yin Earth

76			66	56		46		
庚 Yang Metal			戊 Yang Earth	丁 Yin Fire		丙 Yang Fire		
寅 Tiger			子 Rat	亥 Pig		戌 Dog		
甲 Yang Wood	丙 Yang Fire	戊 Yang Earth	癸 Yin Water	壬 Yang Water	甲 Yang Wood	戊 Yang Earth	辛 Yin Metal	丁 Yin Fire

Instead of seeing his fortunes improve, he broke up with his friends when living in Paris in July 1921. As a result, he was in dire financial straits. In June 1922, he was detained and was interrogated by Albert Sarraut, the French Minister of Colonies. In June 1923, he went to Russia and by 1924, he had returned to China. It had been a frustrating decade for him.

The year 1921 was the year of 辛Yin Metal 酉Rooster. He was then in his 甲Yang Wood 申Monkey luck cycle. The 申Monkey and the 酉Rooster represented the autumn season when metal was at peak strength. For him, metal represented his Friends and enemies. Although there is 壬Yang Water in his 申Monkey luck cycle, the water is not in season in autumn. He would have to wait for his luck to arrive.

In June 1931 he was arrested in Hong Kong and released by December 1932. The year 1931 was the 辛Yin Metal 未Goat year. The 未Goat year harmed his 庚Yang Metal 子Rat day which in turn destroyed his 乙Yin Wood 酉Rooster luck cycle.

The year 1932 was the year of 壬Yang Water 申Monkey. This year brought the壬Yang Water that he needed. It was possible that he might be released.

On 6 January 1933, he was again arrested in Singapore. But this time the detention was brief. The British government in Singapore was eager to get rid of him. On 22 January 1933, he was released in Hong Kong. Although the year was 1933, the Chinese lunar year still considered January to be the twelfth month of 1932. This meant that it was the still the year of壬Yang Water 申Monkey. As he still had the壬Yang Water to assist him, his detention might not last long.

In 1944, he returned to Tonkin when the war seemed lost for Japan. This was the year of 甲Yang Wood 申Monkey which had a Three Harmony relationship with his 庚Yang Metal 子Rat day of birth. However, the Heavenly Stem甲Yang Wood in the year clashed with his庚Yang Metal Heavenly Stem. This indicated that difficulties still lay ahead. He had returned to prepare his people in anticipation of the imminent Japanese defeat. But the French would return after the war to replace the Japanese.

HIS SICKNESS

In July 1945, he was sick with malaria and dysentery. The OSS had sent a force of Americans to work with him. They treated him with quinine and sulfa which probably saved his life. However, Vo Nguyen Giap who was also with him during this period disputed this version of events. He said that the Vietminh contacted an elderly herbalist who treated Ho and helped him to recover.

The year 1945 was the 乙Yin Wood 酉Rooster year. This structure already represented a clash between the乙Yin wood Heavenly Stem and the 辛Yin Metal in the 酉Rooster year. The 酉Rooster year had a destruction relationship with his 子Rat day master. The乙Yin Wood Heavenly Stem in the year combined with his庚Yang Metal Heavenly Stem on his day of birth that resulted in metal. As the酉Rooster year was already strong in metal, the arrival of more metal did not augur well for him. In any case, he was already a strong metal person.

The malaria infected the liver and the red blood cells. In the study of Chinese medicine, the liver was represented by the wood element. The wood element clashed with his metal day master.

The month of July 1945 was the 癸Yin Water 未Goat month. The未Goat was the tomb of wood. As the wood was weak and the metal was strong, the metal element would prevail.

Ho was then aged 55 and in his luck cycle of 丙Yang Fire 戌Dog. The戌Dog had a bullying punishment and destruction relationship with the未Goat month. It was the 戌Dog luck cycle that caused the health problems when it encountered the未Goat month in the酉 Rooster year. When the metal in the戌Dog met the wood in the未 Goat, it brought about disharmony in his chart.

But if the 未Goat was the tomb of wood, then the戌Dog was the tomb of fire. The three elements involved in these relationships were fire, metal and wood. The fire was too weak during the戌Dog luck cycle to control the metal. The wood was also weak during the 未Goat month.

Metal was strong during the酉Rooster year. The酉Rooster had a harm relationship with the戌Dog. This meant that the metal in the酉Rooster harmed the metal in the戌Dog. Therefore, the only element that was strong was the metal element.

If this period was unfavourable to Ho, why did he recover? Perhaps one possible answer was that although there were unfavourable relationships in his chart at this period, it was not dangerous enough to kill him. Another plausible answer was that he had the will to overcome his sickness and continue to live. After all, he had a strong will and something to live for. In the practice of Chinese medicine, the physician took into account the energy and spirit of the patient. His Western counterpart would scoff at such intangible matters, which cannot be examined under the microscope or detected by the stethoscope or by X-rays. Sometimes, we cannot over analyse a given situation. There may not be any straight forward answer. It could also be the fickleness of Fate.

HIS SUCCESS AT DIEN BIEN PHU

The battles at Dien Bien Phu raged from 13 March to 6 May 1954. The year 1954 was the year of 甲 Yang Wood 午 Horse. Ho was then aged 64 and still in his luck cycle of 丁 Yin Fire 亥 Pig. The 亥 Pig brought the much needed 壬 Yang Water. But his luck cycle of the 亥 Pig would be over in 1956 when he reached the age of 66.

He launched his land reform program from March 1955 until August 1956. The program was generally regarded as a failure. The year 1955 was the year of 乙 Yin Wood 未 Goat. The 未 Goat year harmed his 子 Rat day master. By then, he was in his 丁 Yin Fire 亥 Pig luck cycle. The 亥 Pig luck cycle combined with the 未 Goat year that resulted in the wood element. The strong wood weakened the water in his 子 Rat day master. Water represented his abilities and talents. The wood represented his wealth.

In this case, his aim was not to accumulate personal wealth. His program tried to redistribute the land to the farmers. But in doing so, many unscrupulous persons took advantage to settle personal scores with the landowners and exterminated them. As Ho Chi Minh was the leader, the blame for the miscarriage of the program fell on him.

By the time the land reform program was abolished in 1956, he was in his 戊 Yang Earth 子 Rat luck cycle. The year 1956 was the year of 丙 Yang Fire 申 Monkey. The 子 Rat luck cycle had a half combination relationship with the 申 Monkey year that resulted in the water element. This made the water element stronger and restored some stability to the program.

In the public mind, it seemed that it was Ho Chi Minh's iron will that stood in the way of the American intervention in Vietnam. Yet when we analyse the chart of Ho, we find that his best period coincided with Dien Bien Phu. By the time the American involvement in Vietnam began to escalate in the two years before President Kennedy's assassination, Ho's influence in his Party had already declined. His health would also decline in the near future. Therefore, it was more meaningful to focus on Dien Bien Phu rather than on the Vietnam War.

HIS DECLINE *BEFORE* THE VIETNAM WAR

His influence declined during his last decade from the age of 66 when his luck cycle of 戊Yang Earth 子Rat commenced. The 壬Yang Water that was inside the preceding 亥Pig luck cycle was no longer available to him. Ho remained president but authority was delegated to Le Duan who retained power after Ho's death in 1969.

Ho discussed the conduct of the war with his generals but he did not interfere with military campaigns. Although he was the leader of North Vietnam, he did not play an active role in the conduct of the Vietnam War against the Americans. The Americans increased their military advisers but only began to pour in troops from around 1962-63 onwards. By then, both Ho's influence and health had declined.

THE FINAL CURTAIN

Ho died on a 庚Yang Metal 辰 day Dragon in the 申Monkey month. When we examine the chart on the day of his death, we find that the metal element is excessively strong. As the 申Monkey month represented autumn, metal was already strong. However, there was also metal present in the 酉Rooster year and 巳Snake hour. He was a strong metal person. The overly strong metal did not favour a strong metal day master.

Ho Chi Minh Date of death 2-9-1969

时Hour	日Day	月Month	年Year
辛 Yin Metal	庚 Yang Metal	壬 Yang Water	己 Yin Earth
巳 Snake	辰 Dragon	申 Monkey	酉 Rooster
丙　戊　庚 Yang Yang Yang Fire Earth Metal	戊　乙　癸 Yang Yin Yin Earth Wood Water	庚　壬　戊 Yang Yang Yang Metal Water Earth	辛 Yin Metal

In 1973, Henry Kissinger and Le Duc Tho were nominated for the Nobel Prize for Peace. Le Duc Tho declined, saying that "peace had not yet come to my country."

Ho Chi Minh did not live to see the fall of Saigon on 30 April 1975. But Le Duan could not unite the two Vietnams due to their different cultural traditions. Instead, he pursued a war with Cambodia from 1978 to 1979. He wanted to build Vietnam into a regional communist power. His aggressive stance provoked China to launch a border invasion in February 1979. After Le Duan's death in July 1986, Nguyen Van Linh withdrew the army from Cambodia in 1989. Peace had finally come to the paddy fields of Vietnam.

CHAPTER EIGHT

WHATEVER HAPPENED TO PRINCES LEIA? THE PROMISING CAREER OF CARRIE FISHER THAT NEVER FLOURISHED

"May the Force be with you."
(George Lucas, *"Star Wars"*, 1977)

THE DESCENT

*C*arrie Fisher was born on 21 October 1956 to famous parents. Her father was Eddie Fisher and her mother was Debbie Reynolds. When she was two years old, her parents divorced. Her father had been the best man at the wedding of Elizabeth Taylor to her third husband, Mike Todd in 1957. When Mike Todd was killed in the crash of his private aircraft in 1958, Eddie Fisher comforted Elizabeth Taylor in her grief before marrying the widow in 1959. Fans of Debbie Reynolds were outraged at Elizabeth Taylor for breaking up her marriage to Eddie Fisher.

About a year later, Debbie Reynolds married shoe magnate Harry Karl. Unfortunately, her second husband squandered away his fortune and her savings as well. Debbie Reynolds had to continue working and she brought her children, Carrie and Todd Fisher with her whenever she was performing in Vegas and Reno.

At the age of 13, Carrie Fisher began acting in nightclubs. She made her film debut in *"Shampoo"* in 1975 at the age of 19. Her break came in 1977 when she got the role of Princess Leia in *"Star Wars"*. She reprised her role in *"The Empire Strikes Back" in* 1980 and *"Return of the Jedi"* in 1983.

It should have been the start of a promising career. However, it was not mean to be. She was aged 27 when she made her last appearance as Princess Leia in 1983. She dated Paul Simon from 1977 to 1983. But in 1980, she was briefly engaged with Dan Aykroyd. In August 1983, she married Paul Simon. The couple divorced in July 1984. After the divorce, they continued their relationship as friends.

From 1978 until 1984, she became a drug abuser at the age of 22 to 28. It was a wonder how she managed to act in the three *"Star Wars"* movies which were shot during this period.

After her divorce from Paul Simon in 1984, she went into rehabilitation. She wrote her autobiographical novel, *"Postcards from the Edge"* in 1987. She probably found it too difficult to be candid about the events in her life so she disguised it as fiction. That did not prevent the book from becoming a national bestseller.

In 1992, she had an affair with the talent agent, Bryan Lourd. Their relationship ended when he left her not for another woman but for another man. Before they parted ways, their daughter was born in July 1992.

In 1997, she had a psychotic breakdown. She was diagnosed with bi-polar disorder. In 2001, she managed to recover and stabilise. In 2003, she had an affair with James Blunt. In 2005, she took drugs again.

AN ANALYSIS OF THE SURVIVOR

Carrie Fisher was born on a 辛Yin Metal day which is seated on the 酉Rooster. Inside the酉Rooster, there is also辛Yin Metal. This means that her metal day master is already rooted in the酉 Rooster. She was born in the month of the戌Dog. The 戌Dog represented late autumn when metal is strong. So her metal day master is considered strong.

Carrie Fisher 21-10-1956

时 Hour	日 Day	月 Month			年 Year		
甲 Yang Wood	辛 Yin Metal	戊 Yang Earth			丙 Yang Fire		
午 Horse	酉 Rooster	戌 Dog			申 Monkey		
丁　　己 Yin　　Yin Fire　Earth	辛 Yin Metal	戊 Yang Earth	辛 Yin Metal	丁 Yin Fire	庚 Yang Metal	壬 Yang Water	戊 Yang Earth

The elements she needed the most were 壬 Yang Water and 甲 Yang Wood. She has the 壬 Yang Water in her 申 Monkey year. She also has the 甲 Yang Wood in the Heavenly Stem above her 午 Horse hour. Yet despite a promising start in three *"Star Wars"* movies, her career faded away. Instead of pursuing her acting career, she was distracted by drugs. Why did this happen?

Although she has the 甲 Yang Wood in her chart, this wood is too weak in autumn to assist her. There are no roots for the 甲 Yang Wood in any of her 午 Horse hour, 酉 Rooster day, and 戌 Dog month or 申 Monkey year. The wood is already weak enough. When the wood has no roots, it is weakened further to the extent that this wood cannot help her.

The only element that could help her was the 壬 Yang Water in her 申 Monkey year of birth. But the 壬 Yang Water in her 申 Monkey year was too far away from her 酉 Rooster day of birth to assist her. As the year pillar represented childhood, this meant that the 申 Monkey year could benefit her only during her childhood years.

However, she was in her luck cycle of 丙 Yang Fire 申 Monkey from the age of 14 until 23. The presence of the 申 Monkey helped to bring some stability to her wayward behaviour. She was still able to turn up at the studio and act in the first "Star Wars" movie.

Carrie Fisher Luck Cycle

34	24	14	4
甲 Yang Wood	乙 Yin Wood	丙 Yang Fire	丁 Yin Fire
午 Horse	未 Goat	申 Monkey	酉 Rooster
丁　　己 Yin　Yin Fire　Earth	己　　丁　　乙 Yin　Yin　Yin Earth　Fire　Wood	庚　　壬　　戊 Yang　Yang　Yang Metal　Water　Earth	辛 Yin Metal

74	64	54	44
庚 Yang Metal	辛 Yin Metal	壬 Yang Water	癸 Yin Water
寅 Tiger	卯 Rabbit	辰 Dragon	巳 Snake
甲　　丙　　戊 Yang　Yang　Yang Wood　Fire　Earth	乙 Yin Wood	戊　　乙　　癸 Yang　Yin　Yin Earth　Wood　Water	丙　　戊　　庚 Yang　Yang　Yang Fire　Earth　Metal

But the downside was that the壬Yang Water also represented her rebellious streak. This might cause her to go against the establishment or experiment with drugs.

The other two *"Star Wars"* movies were released in 1980 and 1983. By then, she was no longer in her申Monkey luck cycle but in her乙Yin Wood未Goat luck cycle. There was no壬Yang Water in the未Goat luck cycle that could help her. The未Goat represented the summer season when there was no water. How did she manage to complete the filming of the remaining two movies if she was high on drugs during this period?

In 1980, the year of庚Yang Metal 申Monkey arrived. The申 Monkey year brought the 壬Yang Water back to stabilize her life and complete the second instalment, *The Empire Strikes Back.*

The year 1983 was the year of 癸Yin Water 亥Pig. There is 壬Yang Water inside the亥Pig. This meant that she could also complete the third movie *"Return of the Jedi"* this year.

But the 亥Pig year had a combination relationship with her 未 Goat luck cycle that resulted in the wood element. The 未Goat is said to be the storage of wood. The wood element represented her boyfriend or husband star. When this star entered the storage period, she would have problems in her romantic relationships. In 1983 she married Paul Simon. It was not a good year for her to marry. The marriage lasted only one year before their divorce in 1984.

She relapsed into drugs in 2005. This was the year of the乙 Yin Wood酉Rooster. She was then aged 49 and in her luck cycle of 癸Yin Water 巳Snake. The 酉Rooster combined with her 巳 Snake luck cycle to result in the metal element. As she was already a strong metal person, it was not favourable for her metal to be further strengthened.

There could be two major contributory factors that caused her to indulge in drugs. The first had to do with parental neglect; the second was her mixing with the wrong company. Both factors were due to human choice rather than due to Fate. She did not turn to drugs because of her marriage and romantic problems with men. On the contrary, after she divorced Paul Simon in 1984, she went into drug rehabilitation.

Her mother was represented by earth and her father was represented by wood. The earth is abundant in her chart. There is 戊Yang Earth in her 戌Dog month. The戌Dog month represented the parent's pillar. Since the mother's star is in the parents' pillar, she felt the influence of the mother more than the father. The 甲 Yang Wood is present only in the Heavenly Stem above her 午Horse hour. She barely saw her father.

She was born on a 辛Yin Metal day. Her metal was the strongest element in her birth chart. This metal can also represent Friends or competitors. There is metal inside her 酉Rooster day, 戌Dog month and 申Monkey year. She would have Friends throughout her life. But would her Friends benefit her or betray her? As events turned out, she mixed with the wrong company and indulged in drugs.

What does the future hold for her? She was in her luck cycle of 壬Yang Water辰Dragon from the age of 54. The辰Dragon had a combination relationship with her 酉Rooster day of birth that resulted in the metal element. As she was already a strong metal person, it would not be favourable for her to encounter more metal. She would continue to encounter turbulence in her life.

Apart from her drug addiction problems, the underlying reason why her acting career never took off was that she was born in the 戌Dog month. To a 辛Yin Metal person, the fame star was represented by丁Yin Fire. The戌Dog was the storage of fire. When her fame star was in the storage stage, it was considered weak. Even if she was not bogged down by drug issues, she was not likely to become a major actress.

But she was a survivor. If her acting career floundered, she found a second career as a writer. To date, she has written five books and they have been well received. Her *"Postcards from the Edge"* did reasonably well in 1987 for a first book. In 1990, she used a pseudonym to write *"Surrender the Pink"* which dealt with her brief marriage to Paul Simon. She followed it up with *"Delusions of Grandma"* in 1993. Her next novel was *"The Best Awful"* which appeared in 2005. Finally, she was confident enough to publish a no holds barred autobiography, *"Wishful Drinking"* in 2008. At the time of writing this article, her books were still available from Simon and Schuster.

There were other movie stars who made their names but had to struggle with drug problems. Judy Garland and John Belushi were contemporaries of Carrie Fisher. They were far more famous than Carrie Fisher but they did not live long enough to enjoy their success. Judy Garland died of a drug overdose in 1969 at the age of 47. John Belushi followed likewise in 1982 but he died at the much younger age of 33.

Carrie Fisher may not have been a first rate movie star. But unlike the others who descended into drugs, she was a survivor. In choosing to tell her tale, she found success as a writer. There are many possible and varied paths to Success.

The Roman poet Virgil was writing in another context when he said, *"Furor arma ministrat"* ("Anger supplies the arms"). But these words could just as aptly sum up Carrie Fisher's life and achievements.

CHAPTER NINE

HE DID NOT HAVE A SINGLE SPARK OF FIRE IN HIS CHART. HOW DID ALBERT CAMUS EVER WIN THE NOBEL PRIZE?

"What is a rebel? A man who says no . . ."
(from Albert Camus, *"The Rebel"*)

FIRE AND WATER

*I*n the study of Chinese astrology, the elements of fire and water are considered as polarities. They are said to be essential in any given birth chart. Both the fire of the sun and the water of the rain are essential to sustain life forms. If either element is missing from the birth chart, then the chart is said to be defective.

Albert Camus did not have a single spark of fire in his birth chart. He was born on a water day in the cold freezing season of winter. That made it even more imperative for him to have fire. Despite this serious defect, he won the Nobel Prize for Literature in 1957. He became the second youngest writer to win the Prize at the age of 44, beaten only by Rudyard Kipling who won it at the age of 43 in 1907. Among the other contenders he beat were Boris Pasternak and Samuel Beckett, both of whom would win the Prize later.

How could a person with such a birth chart ever have any achievement, let alone win the Nobel Prize? Was there some exception to the rule that one must have both fire and water in his birth chart?

Yet after winning the Prize money of $42,000 (18.77 million francs at that time), he temporarily withdrew from writing any more fiction. Instead, he concentrated on theatre. He tried to get his plays, *"The Possessed" ("Les Possedes")* and *"Caligula"* performed.

After the Prize had made him famous, his views on the Algerian question were sought by the media. He did not agree that Algeria should seek independence. He hoped that Algerians and Moroccans could live together. He condemned the bombings by Algerians and the crackdowns by the French army in Algeria. These views endeared him to neither side. Instead, both sides condemned him.

It seemed that winning the Prize only brought him even more trouble than before.

HIS UNEVENTFUL LIFE

Albert Camus was born on 7 November 1913 in Mondovi near Bone. Bone (later Annaba) was French Algeria's main port near Tunisia. His father was Lucien Auguste Camus who worked at a vineyard. His father died on 11 October 1914 from shrapnel wounds during the Battle of the Marne. He was posthumously awarded the *Croix de Guerre* and *Medaille Militaire*. As a result, his mother was forced to bring her children back to live with their maternal grandmother. His grandmother was Catherine Sintes. They lived in poverty. His mother could not get the state pension as a war widow until 1920. In December 1930 or early January 1931, he showed the first symptoms of tuberculosis. In 1931, his maternal grandmother died.

In 1931, he met his first serious lover, Simone Hie. He managed to enter the first year of university in 1933 due to the financial assistance of his future mother-in-law. In June 1934, he married Simone. But the couple spent their wedding night apart, each of them sleeping at their respective mother's house.

In 1935, he began keeping notebooks and writing his thoughts in them. These notebooks would later be published as a series of *"Carnets"* from 1935 to 1959.

In 1935, he joined the French Communist Party. It was a short lived membership. In 1937, he was expelled from the Party.

From September 1936, he lived apart from Simone who relapsed into drugs. In 1937, he wrote his essay *"Betwixt and Between"* (*"L'envers et l'endroit."*), sometimes also translated as (*"The Wrong Side and the Right Side".*) In July 1939, he met Francine Faure. He began to discuss divorce proceedings with Simone. In 1938, he moved to Paris. The Second World War broke out in September 1939. By May 1940, France had fallen to the advancing German armies. In 1941, he married Francine.

During the war years, he did his part for the Resistance by writing for *Combat* from October 1943 to January 1947. Due to his poor health, he could not have physically fought for the French Resistance. When *Combat* changed to being a daily publication, he ceased writing. In 1949, his tuberculosis returned and he had to live alone for two years.

In November 1954, the war for independence broke out in Algeria. It would drag on until July 1962. Albert Camus would not live long enough to see the end of the Algerian War of Independence.

HIS LITERARY WORKS

In 1936, he wrote *"A Happy Death"* (*"Le Mort heureuse".*) It was his first novel but it would be published posthumously. In 1942, he wrote *"The Outsider"* (*"L'Etranger"*) and *"The Myth of Sisyphus"*

("Le Mythe de Sisyphe"). In "The Myth of Sisyphus", he argued that Man's existence was Absurd since God did not exist and Man was alone in the Universe. The only philosophical question then was whether or not Man should commit suicide. He argued that suicide was not a solution. He pursued this theme further in *"The Rebel"* (*"L'Homme revolte"*) in 1951.

In 1947, he wrote *"The Plague"("La Peste")* which won him the *Prix des Critiques*. This novel was based on a plague that broke out in Oran in the 1940s. Some critics have considered the plague to be an allegory of the Nazi occupation in France during the war. But that would be reading the novel at a literal level. In 1956, he wrote his novel, *"The Fall" ("La Chute.")* In 1945, his play *"Caligula"* was first performed. In 1956, he wrote his play, *"The Possessed" ("Les Possedes")* based on the novel of the same name by Fyodor Dostoevsky.

On 16 October 1957, he was informed that he had won the Nobel Prize for Literature. He was not pleased and said that it should have been awarded to Andre Malraux. In August 1952, he quarrelled with Jean Paul Sartre.

"PUBLIC SILENCE" AFTER THE NOBEL PRIZE

After winning the Nobel Prize, he occupied himself more with the theatre than with writing. He wanted to see his play *"Les Possedes"* performed. He had cut it from his original version of 65 scenes which would have required some 5 hours of performance. His abridged version still had 8 scenes and required 28 actors. In view of the cost of production, the play did not make money. His next play, *"Caligula"* did not fare well.

He was asked about the Algerian issue. He replied that he did not support terrorism whether by the Algerian rebels or the French troops. He hoped that both Moroccans and French could co-exist.

In *"Albert Camus: A Biography"* (Picador, 1979), his biographer, Herbert Lottman, has described the period after winning the Nobel Prize as one of "Public Silence and Private Activity".

HIS ACCIDENT

In January 1960, he had bought a round trip ticket from Lourmarin to Paris. On 4 January 1960, he agreed to follow his editor, Michel Gallimard in his car instead of travelling by train. Gallimard was driving his Facel Vega and Camus was seated in the front right seat. Behind them were seated Gallimard's wife, Janine, their daughter, Anne and their dog, Floc, a Skye terrier. Near the village of Petit-Villeblevin, the car skidded and crashed into a plane tree, then smashed into a second tree some forty feet down the road.

He was thrown backwards and broke his neck. His editor was also killed in the crash. His briefcase contained the incomplete draft of *"The First Man" ("La premier home.")*

Later, investigations revealed that the driver was not driving fast at the time of the accident. The cause of the crash was found to be a burst tyre.

AN ANALYSIS OF A WET AND COLD CHART

Albert Camus was born on a 壬Yang Water 辰Dragon day in the cold winter month of the 亥Pig. This makes his壬Yang Water day master very strong. He badly needed the 丙Yang Fire of the sun to warm his frozen chart. But he did not have any fire in his chart, not even the 丁Yin Fire of the candle. His chart is already too cold. If there is not a single spark of fire to warm it, several conclusions may be drawn. The person would suffer from health problems all his life.

Albert Camus 7-11-1913

时 Hour	日 Day	月 Month	年 Year
辛 Yin Metal	壬 Yang Water	癸 Yin Water	癸 Yin Water
丑 Ox	辰 Dragon	亥 Pig	丑 Ox
己 癸 辛 Yin Yin Yin Earth Water Metal	戊 乙 癸 Yang Yin Yin Earth Wood Water	壬 甲 Yang Yang Water Wood	己 癸 辛 Yin Yin Yin Earth Water Metal

He would be prone to water related sickness such as tuberculosis. The person tended to have a gloomy, melancholic outlook on life. Fire represented, among other things, joy and anger. He would be less likely to find happiness in his lifetime. For a male born on a water day, fire represented his women and his wealth. The absence of fire does not necessarily mean that he cannot find female friends or get married. But he was not that interested in women and was not likely to become a womaniser.

HIS WOMEN

Despite the absence of women stars in his birth chart, he married twice and raised a family from the second marriage. How to explain the apparent discrepancy? He married his first wife, Simone Hie, in 1934. This was the year of the 甲 Yang Wood 戌 Dog. The 戌 Dog represented autumn season when metal was strong. However, there is also 丁 Yin Fire inside the 戌 Dog. The fire represented his women. He had the opportunity to meet women during this year. But since the fire was not strong in autumn, the passion would not last long or the romantic feelings would not be so strong.

From 1936, he began to live apart from Simone. This was the year of 丙 Yang Fire 子 Rat. Although there was fire, the fire had no roots in the 子 Rat. The 子 Rat was the height of winter when the water element was at peak strength. The fire element was therefore very weak. Whatever weak passions that had existed between the couple during the early years of the marriage had died down by this year.

Albert Camus Luck Cycle

40	30	20	10
己 Yin Earth	庚 Yang Metal	辛 Yin Metal	壬 Yang Water
未 Goat	申 Monkey	酉 Rooster	戌 Dog
己　丁　乙 Yin　Yin　Yin Earth　Fire　Wood	庚　壬　戊 Yang　Yang　Yang Metal　Water　Earth	辛 Yin Metal	戊　辛　丁 Yang　Yin　Yin Earth　Metal　Fire

80	70	60	50
乙 Yin Wood	丙 Yang Fire	丁 Yin Fire	戊 Yang Earth
卯 Rabbit	辰 Dragon	巳 Snake	午 Horse
乙 Yin Wood	戊　乙　癸 Yang　Yin　Yin Earth　Wood　Water	丙　戊　庚 Yang　Yang　Yang Fire　Earth　Metal	丁　己 Yin　Yin Fire　Earth

In July 1939, he began to discuss divorce proceedings with Simone because he had met Francine Faure and wanted to marry her. The year 1939 was the year of 己Yin Earth 卯Rabbit. The卯 Rabbit clashed with his 酉Rooster luck cycle.

In 1941, he got his wish and married Francine Faure in the year of 辛Yin Metal 巳Snake. As the 巳Snake represented summer, fire would be strong during this year. He would probably become involved in women this year.

THE BREAK-UP AND THE FAME

In August 1952, he quarrelled with Jean Paul Sartre which led to their breakup. This quarrel occurred during the year of the 壬 Yang Water 辰Dragon. The辰Dragon year had a self-punishment relationship with his辰Dragon day of birth. As the壬Yang Water represented his Friends, it was possible that he might do something that led to an argument or even breakup with his Friends.

In 1957, he won the Nobel Prize in the year of 丁Yin Fire 酉 Rooster. The酉Rooster year had a combination relationship with his 辰Dragon day of birth that resulted in metal. The metal element produced his water day master. This meant that his resources were strong in that year. There was a possibility that he might find success or be recognised.

His fame element was 戊Yang Earth but the earth element was not strong during the酉Rooster year. The酉Rooster represented the autumn season when the metal element was at peak strength which in turn exhausted the earth. Although he was nominated for the Nobel Prize, there were other worthy nominees such as Boris Pasternak and Samuel Beckett.

THE WRITER AND THE WOULD-BE PLAYWRIGHT

When we examine the years when his major works were published, one pattern seemed to emerge. All his major works were produced during the years when fire was present.

In 1937, the year of 丁Yin Fire 丑Ox, he wrote *"The Right Side and the Wrong Side" ("L'envers et endroit.")* In 1942, he wrote *"The Myth of Sisyphus" ("Le Mythe de Sisiyphe")* and *"The Outsider" ("L'Etranger")*. This was the year of the壬Yang Water 午Horse. In 1947, he wrote *"The Plague" ("La Peste")* during the year of the丁 Yin Fire 亥Pig. In 1956, he wrote *"The Fall" ("La Chute")* in the year of 丙Yang Fire 申Monkey. In 1957, the year of 丁Yin Fire 酉 Rooster, he wrote *"Exile and the Kingdom" ("L'exil et le royaume.")*

In all the above mentioned years, there was the fire element either in the Heavenly Stem or the Earthly Branch. This validated

123

the theory that one must have both the elements of fire and water—if not in the birth chart, then at least in the luck cycles or year pillars—in order to have some potential for success in life.

In 1959 his play *"The Possessed" ("Les Possedes")* was performed in the year of 已 Yin Earth 亥 Pig. There was no fire present during this year. This play has not been considered one of his major works.

If he had only written plays, he would probably have been forgotten today. In order to write plays successfully, it could be argued that one must have the fire element present in his birth chart. How do we justify this rationale?

A playwright writes plays to be performed, unlike a novelist whose works are meant to be read. One of the characteristics of fire is that the bright flames of the fire can easily be seen from afar. In other words, fire is meant to be seen just like a play is meant to be performed in front of an audience. Therefore, in order to be a successful playwright, he needed some spark of fire in his birth chart.

Camus may have been a creative writer but he was a poor playwright. A successful dramatist should have a sense of drama. Camus did not. His birth chart did not have a single spark of fire. He lacked the vitality, the suspense and theatrics that can make a good dramatist. In his novels and essays, he can afford to be brooding and introspective, which after all was what he excelled in. In these works, his outlook was generally pessimistic but not to the point of despair or suicide.

The fire element is associated with the element of joy. When a person lacked the fire element in his birth chart, he will find it harder to find happiness or adopt a more optimistic viewpoint.

AN ANALYSIS OF HIS ACCIDENT

The accident occurred on a 辛 Yin Metal 卯 Rabbit day. The 卯 Rabbit day had a Three Harmony relationship with the 亥 Pig year and the 未 Goat hour on the day of the accident that resulted in the wood element. This meant that the wood element was very strong on that day.

Albert Camus accident 4-1-1960

时Hour	日Day	月Month	年Year
乙 Yin Wood	辛 Yin Metal	丁 Yin Fire	己 Yin Earth
未 Goat	卯 Rabbit	丑 Ox	亥 Pig
己　丁　乙 Yin　Yin　Yin Earth Fire Wood	乙 Yin Wood	己　癸　辛 Yin　Yin　Yin Earth Water Metal	壬　　甲 Yang　Yang Water　Wood

The accident occurred in the 丑Ox month which represented the winter season. The wood element is said to be in the growth stage during the winter season because water produced wood. This season further strengthened the wood. The 卯Rabbit day also had a partial combination relationship with the亥Pig birth month of Camus. This partial or half combination also resulted in the wood element.

The卯Rabbit day had a harm relationship with the 辰Dragon day of birth of Camus. This meant that the day of the accident was a potentially dangerous day for him.

The 丑Ox month of the day of the accident clashed with the 未 Goat luck cycle of Camus. This丑Ox month also clashed with the 未Goat hour on the day of the accident. In addition, this未Goat hour also clashed with the丑Ox year of birth and丑Ox hour of birth of Camus. The various clashes between the丑Ox and the未 Goat do not bode well for him. He would have been well advised to postpone his journey to another day.

In Chinese medicine, the neck is represented by the 乙Yin Wood element. There was辛Yin Metal on the Heavenly Stem on the卯Rabbit day of the accident. This symbolised the clash between the metal and the wood element. Although the wood element was very strong on the day of the accident, there was the potential threat of the metal chopping the wood.

In the accident, Camus was thrown backwards and broke his neck. He also suffered other injuries but this injury was serious enough to kill him.

If Camus had survived the accident, would he have had more achievements? Perhaps but he would have to wait until the age of 60 to see any substantial success. He needed fire, especially 丙 Yang Fire. He was then in his luck cycle of 未 Goat. If he had lived, his next luck cycle would have been 午 Horse from the age of 50, followed by the 巳 Snake luck cycle from the age of 60. The 未 Goat, the 午 Horse and the 巳 Snake represent summer season which brings the fire that Camus so badly needed in his chart. However, only the 巳 Snake has the 丙 Yang Fire that he required. The 未 Goat and the 午 Horse only contain the 丁 Yin Fire which is not warm enough to bring the heat that Camus needed. That was why he would have to live until the age of 60 to see any lasting success.

However, even if he had lived longer, he would probably have to endure his illness longer. A longer life did not necessarily mean a happier life or a better life. His birth chart was too wet and cold without any fire. He would have to struggle with sickness throughout his life. Perhaps it was more merciful that his life was cut short by an accident.

"MY NAME IS BOND . . . JAMES BOND." HOW THE UNREAL SPY WORLD MADE REAL MONEY FOR IAN FLEMING

"I am going to write the spy story to end all spy stories."
(Ian Fleming, circa 1952)

THE ADVANTAGES IN HIS EARLY LIFE

Despite being born into a wealthy and influential family in May 1908, Ian Lancaster Fleming had no achievements until the age of 31. He was the second of four sons born to Valentine Fleming and Evelyn St. Croix Rose. His father had been Conservative Member of Parliament for Henley in 1910. Fleming grew up under the shadow of his precocious elder brother, Peter. In May 1917, his father, Major

Valentine Fleming was killed by artillery fire in the First World War. It was a shock to the boys who idolised their father. Fleming would show respect to older men for the rest of his life as though they were his father figures.

He began studying at the elite public school, Eton, from the age of 13. He did not do well in school except in sports when he became *Victor Ludorum* or school sports champion. His mother took him away from Eton at the age of 17, one term earlier. She sent him to a tutorial crammer as preparation for entry to the Royal Military Academy, Sandhurst. He did not make the grade as a cadet at Sandhurst either. He had an affair with the colonel's daughter. When she turned him down as partner to attend a ball, he visited a local brothel and contracted gonorrhoea.

THE LOST YEARS

His exasperated mother tried to prepare him for a career in the Foreign Office. He was sent to the Tennerhof, a finishing school at Kitzbuhel, Austria. This school was run by an English couple, Ernan and Phyllis Forbes Dennis. The husband was an ex-diplomat and spy, the wife was a novelist. Fleming learnt skiing and had affairs with the local girls. He learnt French and German. He also spent two years in Munich and Geneva. He developed a liking for fast cars, fast women and expensive living. He became engaged to Monique Panchard de Bottomes. His mother disapproved and that was the end of the engagement.

In 1931, he sat for the Foreign Office examinations but failed to qualify. In despair, his mother arranged for him to work at Reuters News Agency in October 1931. In 1933, he was sent to Moscow to cover the trial of some Vickers engineers. Here he had the temerity to seek an interview with Stalin. He was surprised to receive a note, apparently signed by Stalin, saying he was too busy.

In October 1933, Fleming abandoned journalism which he seemed to enjoy for a boring job at the merchant bank, Cull & Co. He did not do well in this job either. In 1935, he joined a stockbroking firm. He was a bad stockbroker and spent money lavishly on women he met at his clubs. He lived the life of a lothario who was rapidly ruining himself.

THE FORMATIVE YEARS WITH NAVAL INTELLIGENCE

Then he had lunch with Rear Admiral John Godfrey on 24 May 1939. The Admiral was then Director of Naval Intelligence. He was looking for an assistant and decided to hire Fleming. Fleming joined Naval Intelligence with the rank of Lieutenant (the equivalent of Captain in the army). This was quite a high rank considering that Fleming had failed to obtain a commission at Sandhurst.

Rear Admiral Godfrey was an irascible and unpopular man in the Admiralty. He used Fleming as his liaison with other parts of British intelligence. Fleming already had shown respect for older men so he could deal with the older, self-important men he met in the course of his duties. He also had the gambler's instinct for adventure. When the Second World War broke out in September 1939, he would begin his spy career in earnest. At the age of 31, Fleming was in his element.

During the war, he only planned missions. He was not allowed to fight in the front lines because he knew too much and could not risk getting caught. On 19 August 1942, the 2nd Canadian Infantry Division assaulted the port of Dieppe in "*Operation Jubilee.*" Fleming was on board *HMS Fernie*, a Hunt class destroyer, watching the raid. He was allowed to follow a Royal Marine commando detachment from *HMS Locust*. But flank landings at Puys and Pourville were pinned down by the defences on the headlands overlooking the town and the beachhead. The launch of the second wave was cancelled. Some artillery shells hit *HMS Fernie*, killing one sailor and injuring several others. That was the extent of Fleming's experience in combat. He had not even fired any weapons in anger.

After the war, he returned to journalism by working for the Kemsley newspaper group. He was allowed to spend the winter at Jamaica. In 1945, he built a house at St Mary Parish in Jamaica. He retired in December 1959 and settled down in Jamaica.

Chapter Ten

THE NOVELIST YEARS

He wrote his first novel *"Casino Royale"* in February 1952. He wanted his hero to have the "dullest name possible" so eventually he settled on James Bond. But he could not find a publisher until his brother, Peter Fleming, persuaded Jonathan Cape to publish the book. To the publisher's surprise, the novel sold 4,750 copies. Jonathan Cape offered him a contract for another three books. There would be 12 James Bond novels published until his death in 1964, followed by another two books published posthumously.

In 1954, the TV rights for *"Casino Royale"* were sold to CBS for $1,000 who made a play titled *"Climax."* In 1954, Fleming was commissioned to write a Bond series for CBS but nothing came of it. He met filmmaker Kevin McClory and screenwriter Jack Whittingham. Together, they drafted a story about Bond's underwater adventures in the Caribbean. Fleming used these ideas in his novel *"Thunderball"* which was published in 1961. But McClory and Whittingham claimed that they also contributed to the work and filed a legal suit for breach of copyright. The lawsuit was a long drawn out affair and took a toll on Fleming's health.

In 1959, Fleming published *"Goldfinger."* The architect, Erno Goldfinger, was not amused to see his name used for the villain and threatened to instruct his lawyers to halt publication of the book. Fleming was furious and suggested to his publishers that the name of his villain, Auric Goldfinger, should be changed to Auric Goldprick. The publisher managed to negotiate a truce by suggesting that the name Goldfinger would be used with Auric in the advertisements for the book.

The effect of the *"Goldfinger"* and *"Thunderball"* issues had a debilitating effect on Fleming's already poor health.

HIS WOMEN AND HIS HEALTH

He had a cavalier attitude towards women and sex. He had many affairs, usually with other people's wives. He was brash when it came to approaching women. He would blatantly ask a woman he had just met for the first time to go to bed with him. If she was shocked, offended or refused, he merely shrugged and moved on to the next woman.

During the war years, he had an affair with Ann Charteris who was then the wife of Baron O'Neill. At the same time, she also had an affair with Esmond Harmsworth, the heir to Lord Rothermere, the owner of the *"Daily Mail."* After her first husband died during the war, Ann expected Fleming to marry her. But he chose to remain single. In June 1945, Ann Charteris married Viscount Rothermere. In 1951, Viscount Rothermere divorced Ann on the grounds of her affair with Ian Fleming.

In 1948, Ann gave birth to Fleming's daughter, Mary, who died at birth. Fleming finally married Ann Charteris on 24 March 1952. By then, she was already pregnant. Their son, Caspar was born on 12 August 1952. Both of them were openly unfaithful to each other before and during their marriage. He had an affair with Blanche Blackwell, a neighbour in Jamaica. Ann Charteris had an affair with Hugh Gaskell, the leader of the Labour Party.

It was a tempestuous marriage. There were many rows, some of them in public. But despite their affairs with third parties and their differences, they remained married. Perhaps the fact that the marriage endured showed that there was some real affection among the couple. However, the marriage could also have endured because the couple was able to accept each other's infidelities.

He may have based his hero upon his wartime experiences dealing with spies. But ironically, these experiences also made him realise that James Bond was a most improbable spy. To begin with, his cover as a spy was already blown. His enemies knew that he was working for British Intelligence even before they began to fight each other. In any case, James Bond was living a highly conspicuous lifestyle which would have attracted unwanted attention. He was frequently shown spending his time gambling in casinos, frolicking with attractive women, driving expensive cars and using the most outrageous gadgets.

Fleming wrote for about three hours in the morning, typically from 9.30 am to 12.30 pm and one hour in the evening. By following this schedule, he could type about 2,000 words per day. He also said that he never corrected anything nor reviewed what he had written. If he did, he would have been mortified. "How could I write such piffle?"

He knew very well that James Bond could not have survived in the real world of the modern spy. But it did not matter. He modelled James Bond after his own dissolute life style of heavy smoking, drinking, gambling and flirting with women. It would not have been possible for Fleming to model his hero otherwise. The readers and the audience lapped it all up. Why shouldn't they be attracted to a spy who lived the high life funded by His Majesty's government?

But Fleming would pay the ultimate price for his hedonistic lifestyle. He was said to smoke some 70 cigarettes per day and gulped down an entire bottle of gin daily. In 1946, at the age of 38, he suffered serious chest pains which eventually spread to his neck. In 1956, his kidney stones began to fail. In 1961, he had his first heart attack which required one month's stay in the hospital. He had only three more years to live. On 11 August 1964, he suffered another heart attack. He died in the early morning of 12 August 1964 which was also his son's twelfth birthday.

HIS LOST YEARS ANALYSED

Ian Fleming was born on a 癸Yin Water 未Goat day in the month of the巳Snake. As the巳Snake represents summer, this meant that his water was weak. The water has some roots in the 申 Monkey year.

Ian Fleming 28-5-1908

时 Hour?	日 Day	月 Month	年 Year
甲 Yang Wood	癸 Yin Water	丁 Yin Fire	戊 Yang Earth
寅 Tiger	未 Goat	巳 Snake	申 Monkey
甲　丙　戊 Yang　Yang　Yang Wood　Fire　Earth	已　丁　乙 Yin　Yin　Yin Earth　Fire　Wood	丙　戊　庚 Yang　Yang　Yang Fire　Earth　Metal	庚　壬　戊 Yang　Yang　Yang Metal　Water　Earth

There seemed to be some uncertainty over his hour of birth. Some sources say that he was born in the 子 Rat hour while other sources indicate that he was born in the 寅 Tiger hour. We shall need to examine in some detail which is the more likely hour. Based upon the timing of his health issues and the date of his death, we deduced that the 寅 Tiger hour seemed more probable than the 子 Rat hour.

To a male water person, the fire element represented his women and his wealth. The fire element is strong and plentiful in his birth chart. There is fire in the 巳 Snake month and in his 未 Goat day. If his hour of birth is the 寅 Tiger hour, then there is fire in the hour of birth as well. He was a weak water day master. The presence of so much fire and such strong fire could be interpreted to mean that this person would have many affairs with women in his life. If he came into money, he could not control his money. Instead, he might even squander all his money within a short time.

In theory, water controlled fire. But this water is too weak to control the fire. His water day master was born in the wrong season so how could his water be strong? Even if it was assumed that he was born in the 子 Rat hour instead of the 寅 Tiger hour, the 癸 Yin Water inside the 子 Rat hour did not make his water day master strong. It is a logical fallacy to argue that the hour of birth may strengthen or weaken the day master. The strength of the day master is dependent on the season of birth, not upon the hour of birth.

The elements that he needed were 甲Yang Wood, 丙Yang Fire and 癸Yin Water. He only had the丙Yang Fire and 癸Yin Water in his birth chart. There was丙Yang Fire in his巳Snake month. The fire is at peak strength in the summer season. Yet he had no achievement until the age of 45. Why?

His 巳Snake month had both a destruction and punishment relationship with his甲Monkey year. The year represented the childhood stage of life. The month of birth represented youth and early adulthood. The 甲Monkey year contained the 壬Yang Water. This water controlled the 丙Yang Fire inside his 巳Snake month. This nullified the effects of his壬Yang Water. He would have to struggle during his early years despite help from his wealthy and influential mother.

INITIALLY, HIS LUCK IMPROVED . . .

The壬Yang Water that he needed arrived from the age of 43 when he entered his luck cycle of 壬Yang Water 戌Dog. By the time he reached 43 years old, it was the year 1951. In 1952, he began what would become his first novel, *"Casino Royale."* The year 1952 was the year of 壬Yang Water 辰Dragon. If the element that he needed was壬Yang Water, now he had it both in his luck cycle and the annual year pillar! His efforts during this year paid off in spades when he found a publisher and his novel began to sell well. This was a rarity for a newbie fiction writer.

Ian Fleming Luck Cycle

33	23	13	3
辛 Yin Metal	庚 Yang Metal	已 Yin Earth	戊 Yang Earth
酉 Rooster	申 Monkey	未 Goat	午 Horse
辛 Yin Metal	庚 壬 戊 Yang Yang Yang Metal Water Earth	已 丁 乙 Yin Yin Yin Earth Fire Wood	丁 已 Yin Yin Fire Earth

73	63	53	43
乙 Yin Wood	甲 Yang Wood	癸 Yin Water	壬 Yang Water
丑 Ox	子 Rat	亥 Pig	戌 Dog
已 癸 辛 Yin Yin Yin Earth Water Metal	癸 Yin Water	壬 甲 Yang Yang Water Wood	戊 辛 丁 Yang Yin Yin Earth Metal Fire

By 1959, he had published seven James Bond novels, the last being *"Goldfinger."* He could afford to retire from the newspaper group at the age of 51. The year 1959 was the year of 已Yin Earth 亥Pig. But his troubles were only beginning. If there was 壬Yang Water inside the亥Pig, then why did he encounter problems from the architect, Erno Goldfinger?

The previous luck cycle of壬Yang Water 戌Dog meant that the water was located in the autumn season. This water was not so strong compared to the same壬Yang Water located inside the亥Pig which was his next luck cycle from age 53. The亥Pig represented the winter season when water was at peak strength. Furthermore, the戌Dog luck cycle had a Three Harmony relationship with his 寅Tiger hour of birth. The戌Dog luck cycle was more favourable compared to the亥Pig luck cycle even though壬Yang Water was present in both luck cycles. Perhaps this was a good example to illustrate that sometimes theory cannot be applied blindly.

. . . THEN HIS LUCK DECLINED

By the year 1961, he was aged 53 and in his luck cycle of 癸Yin Water 亥Pig. The new luck cycle would bring him legal problems from his next novel, *"Thunderball."* As if that was not enough, his health began to deteriorate. Since he steadfastly refused to heed medical advice, he would be dead within three years. But he was in his luck cycle of亥Pig which brought him the 壬Yang Water that he needed. So how to explain why his luck began to change for the worse instead of for the better?

If he was born in the 寅Tiger hour, then the threat to his health is more substantial than if he were born in the 子Rat hour. The亥 Pig had a combination relationship with the寅Tiger that resulted in the wood element. The wood reduced his weak癸Yin Water day master even further.

His亥Pig luck cycle destroyed his寅Tiger hour which represented his old age from about age 50. The 壬Yang Water inside the亥Pig destroyed the 丙Yang Fire inside the 寅Tiger. This meant that his wealth or his income was affected.

In 1961, the lawsuit over the *"Thunderball"* claims began. This was the year of the 辛Yin Metal丑Ox. The丑Ox year and his 巳 Snake month of birth formed the metal frame together with the 酉 Rooster. Since the酉Rooster was not present in this case, we say that there was a half combination of metal. The metal represented his resources such as his ideas for writing. He became too productive and searched for material to write his next novel. But other people also claimed his resources in the sense that they wanted credit for co-writing the scripts.

Ian Fleming date of death 12-8-1964

时Hour?	日Day			月Month			年Year		
	癸 Yin Water			壬 Yang Water			甲 Yang Wood		
	巳 Snake			申 Monkey			辰 Dragon		
	丙 Yang Fire	戊 Yang Earth	庚 Yang Metal	庚 Yang Metal	壬 Yang Water	戊 Yang Earth	戊 Yang Earth	乙 Yin Wood	癸 Yin Water

THE FINALE

The day of his death was the 癸Yin Water 巳Snake day. The 巳 Snake had an ungrateful punishment and harm relationship with his 寅Tiger hour of birth. The 寅Tiger hour of birth represented his old age. The 申Monkey month of his death also had an ungrateful punishment and destruction relationship with his 巳Snake month of birth. Finally, the 辰Dragon year of death was the tomb of water. The 癸Yin Water was his day of birth so it represented the self. When the self-element entered the tomb, there was some possibility of sickness and in severe cases, perhaps even death.

"THE UNFINISHED SYMPHONY"

What is an unfinished symphony? In Western classical music, an unfinished symphony referred to a work that the composer left unfinished. The reasons why the work was unfinished could vary from sickness, death, plain loss of interest or distracted by other more lucrative work.

The term "unfinished symphony" came into vogue when Franz Peter Schubert (1797-1828) left his Symphony No. 8 in B minor unfinished in 1822. He had written only two out of the four movements that comprised a symphony. Yet he finished his next symphony, No. 9 in C Major which he worked on from 1825 until his death in 1828. His unfinished symphony therefore was not due to an untimely death, unlike Mozart's "*Requiem.*" However, the term "unfinished symphony" has become a generic term for any work of art such as literature besides music that was left unfinished by the artist.

What has an unfinished symphony to do with astrology? In the course of our research, we have come across many cases when the hour of birth was not known. Sometimes, the hour of birth was not known with certainty, that is, there were several sources who gave different hours of birth for the same person.

In these cases, one could have torn his proverbial hair out in despair. The purist astrologer argued that one must have the complete birth data before he could even start to analyse the chart. There were good reasons for this argument. When the hour of birth is not known, the chart is incomplete. The hour of birth could make all the difference between a bad chart and a good chart.

But we do not live in an ideal world. If the hour of birth was not known but the person had contributed in a significant way to society, should we turn our backs and refuse to analyse his chart? If an astrologer had some experience, could he not deduce the hour of birth or at least reduce the possibilities under certain conditions? One condition was that the subject must have lived to a ripe old age. Another condition was that there must be key or pivotal events in his old age. Then we could use the timing of these events to narrow down the probable hours of birth.

Why bother to go through all this trouble? Why not just write about someone else? The simplest answer would be that the subject we proposed to write about held such strong interest for the researcher that he just could not drop the project due to the absence of the hour of birth.

In the next case that we shall look at, the hours of birth of both the father and son were not known. We should classify these cases as our unfinished symphonies.

Since the father lived to 70 years old and there were key events late in his life, it was possible for us to deduce his hour of birth. The same cannot be said for the son. These events occurred when the son was in his thirties. By the time the hullabaloo was over, there was no longer any reason for the public to remain interested in the son.

We commenced our work by discussing the case of a man who had everything in life except children. Perhaps it is fitting to conclude our effort by examining the case of a man who had children but had little reason to cheer towards the end of his life.

AGAINST THE ODDS: THE IMPROBABLE RISE OF WANG LABORATORIES

"I have some special knowledge that the outside world is interested in . . ."
(An Wang, circa 1951 when he was about to start his own company)

THE DECISIONS

If An Wang had been contented to work as an employee for the rest of his working life, he might not have come to grief in his twilight years. Instead, he chose to start his own business in a foreign country. In June 1945, he was a Chinese engineer working for a company in China. When his employer sent a batch of engineers to work in the US, he was among those chosen. The Second World

War was drawing to a close in the Pacific. He decided not to return to China after the Communists came into power in China.

After working for six years, he decided to start his own business under the name Wang Laboratories. The initial years were difficult. However, his company eventually grew so much that he chose to seek public listing in August 1967.

Then he wanted to leave a legacy so he made his elder son, Fred Wang, head of research in October 1983. This appointment signalled the decline of his company. The head of the sales division and three heads of design teams resigned. He ignored the warning signs. In November 1986, he even promoted his son as president of his company. Within three years, in August 1989, he had to dismiss the son he himself had installed. Seven months later, in March 1990, he died a broken hearted man.

How did he end up in such a sorry state of affairs? Was it his Fate? If so, could he not possibly escape his Fate by choosing another fork in the road of Life?

THE BEGINNINGS

An Wang was born on 7 February 1920 to poor parents in China. In July 1935, the Japanese invaded China. Despite the unsettled conditions, he graduated in 1940 at the top of his class in Chiao Tung University, Shanghai. He eventually found employment with the Radio Corporation in Kuielin. The company sent some of their best engineers to work in the US. Naturally, An Wang was one of those selected. They arrived in the US in June 1945. An Wang's parents and older sister had been killed in the war. His three remaining siblings were cared for by relatives. He did not see them again until 40 years later.

In the meantime, he had married. He had to leave his wife behind in China because wives were not allowed by the company to accompany their husbands. He bought a coat in the US which he intended to send to his wife. But his wife divorced him in 1941. Later in his life, he refused to mention or discuss his first wife in his conversations with his family or other people in his company.

In 1947, the Communists overran China. An Wang decided not to return to China. In any case, what was there to return for? His parents were dead, his wife had divorced him, and his remaining siblings did not rely on him for their care. He tried to find an apartment to rent. That was when he encountered the first inklings that Asians such as the Chinese were a minority and not so welcome in the US. He finally found an apartment only after several landlords refused to rent their properties to him.

In June 1948, he obtained a Ph.D. and worked for Harvard Laboratory. In 1949, he married Lorraine Chu. They had two sons, Fred and Courtney, and one daughter, Juliette.

THE COMPANY

He was tired of working for other people and yearned to start his own business. His fellow colleagues tried to dissuade him. They pointed out that as an immigrant, he would face a lot of obstacles. He chose not to listen to their objections. On 30 June 1951, he started Wang Laboratories to make memory cores which he sold for $4.00. The initial years were extremely tough. But he had built up a reputation by then so he had some business.

The company shifted to Tewksbury, Boston in 1963. At first, he wanted to buy only 10 acres of the 72 acres available. Eventually, he changed his mind and bought the entire 72 acres instead. In 1975, the company bought 16 acres of land and a building for $1.85 million in Lowell, Massachusetts. In October 1969 John Cunningham joined the company as head of marketing.

In 1962, his company revenue rose to $427,000. By 1963, revenues had grown to $643,000. In 1964, sales reached $1.4 million. On 23 August 1967, the company went public. The IPO was priced at $12.50. By the close of trading, the share price reached $40.50. The company's stock was worth $70 million on paper. His family's share was worth $50 million. The intention of going public had been to raise $2.5 million.

Fred Wang joined the company on a part-time basis in June 1972. In early 1979, Fred Wang completed his 13 week management development course at Harvard Business School. When he returned, An Wang split up the marketing division. The product planning and development part was given to Fred Wang. The external marketing and advertising part was given to Carl Masi. In October 1983, his father made Fred Wang head of research and development.

On 4 October 1983, Fred Wang announced to the media that the company would launch 14 new products. The senior management knew that most of these products at that time existed only in the imagination. The products were not yet even designed, let alone produced.

An Wang chose to divide his design teams under three groups rather than consolidate them under one head of department. Harold Kaplow was the head of the team that launched the Wang Word Processor in June 1976. Bob Siegel headed the design team that produced the VS minicomputer in 1979. Bob Kolk was the chief of the team that designed the Wang 2200 PC in 1979.

ENTER "BIG BLUE"

In 1983, IBM began mass production of cheap PCs. This was a serious blow to Wang Laboratories. At one stroke, the cheap and popular IBM PC replaced both the Wang 2200 PC and the Wang Word Processor. Wang Laboratories had no effective response to the threat. An Wang had refused to divulge his code and let the Wang PC operate on proprietary systems.

But IBM was savvy enough to let their code be known so that other programmers could write their programs to run on the IBM PC. The Wang PC could use only the Wang Word Processor. The IBM PC could use thousands of programs. The consumers flocked to buy the IBM PC instead of the Wang PC. The IBM PC could be made for as low as $25 each. The Wang PC cost more than the IBM PC so they could not compete on price.

To his credit, Fred Wang's team came up with the Wang Office Assistant to be sold at $2,400. But this program could only run Word Processing. The IBM PC could run many popular programs, including Lotus 1-2-3. Besides, the Wang PC had to use Wang printers only. The IBM PC was compatible with any printer. Wang Laboratories lost about $30 million.

THE RESIGNATIONS

Harold Kaplow was the first design chief to resign from the company in the autumn of 1982. He left even before Fred Wang had been appointed head of research and development in 1983. Bob Siegel was the next to resign in 1984. The last of the design heads to leave was Bob Kolk who left in 1985 for NEC. The three design chiefs whose teams had produced winning products were gone. Their departure left a serious vacuum that was never satisfactorily filled. The company began to lose momentum.

Patricia Seybold said that "Wang Laboratories had lost their vision." Later she would establish her reputation as an IT management consultant with the publication of *"Customers.Com"* (Times Books, 2000) and *"The Customer Revolution"* (Crown Business, 2001).

THE PROBLEMS INTENSIFY

The company had basked in the glory of its products from about 1977 until 1981. The phenomenal growth had hidden the serious problems such as sloppy operations that began from 1979 until 1983. Only insiders such as senior management knew that these problems existed within the company.

By then, Wang Laboratories had an unenviable reputation for late deliveries, poor services and support. When their products were hot and in demand, these weakness were tolerated by the customers. But when their competitors began to offer better products, the consumers no longer had to put up with the delays and the sloppy service. Wang Laboratories could no longer depend on the superiority of their products which had become obsolete. They would never be able to overcome the inferiority of their products compared to their competitors' products.

John Cunningham was so worried that he sold his 140,000 shares in 1983 at about $40.50, near the all-time peak of the share price at $40.60. His wise move meant that he profited about $8.3 million. Other members of the senior management also began to unload their shares. The Securities Commission were so concerned that they started an investigation but could not find any evidence of insider trading.

Sometime in 1985, An Wang told Cunningham that he planned to install his son as president of the company. Cunningham was aghast and asked whether Fred Wang would be a figurehead or would have real power as president. When An Wang replied that his son would have real authority as the president instead of being a mere figurehead, Cunningham saw the writing on the wall. The company's future seemed to be very bleak under the leadership of the son.

DEPARTURE OF "AN AMERICAN SON"

In May 1985, the company laid off 1,600 workers out of 32,000 employees or about 5 % of the workforce. This was the second layoff since the 1970s when the company had to lay off about 40 workers.

John Cunningham resigned on 13 July 1985. It was a sad day for him. He had been with the company since October 1969 when he joined as head of the production department. His resignation took place more than a year before Fred Wang became president of the company on 19 November 1986.

The resignation of John Cunningham was a severe personal blow to An Wang. In his book, *"Riding the Runaway Horse: The Rise and Decline of Wang Laboratories"* (Little, Brown & Co., 1992), Charles Kenney said that the Wang family had come to regard John Cunningham as "an American son."

But Fred Wang would last less than three years as president. By July 1989, the company was in dire financial straits. The father, An Wang, was sick and lying on his hospital bed. On 4 August 1989, the father had to dismiss the son that he himself had installed as president. Less than a year later, he died on 24 March 1990.

THE FATHER

An Wang was born on a 乙 Yin Wood 未 Goat day in the 寅 Tiger month. The 寅 Tiger month represented early spring when wood was strong. Therefore, his wood day master is considered strong because it was born in season.

An Wang 7-2-1920

时 Hour?	日 Day	月 Month	年 Year
丁 Yin Fire	乙 Yin Wood	戊 Yang Earth	庚 Yang Metal
丑 Ox	未 Goat	寅 Tiger	申 Monkey
己 癸 辛 Yin Yin Yin Earth Water Metal	己 丁 乙 Yin Yin Yin Earth Fire Wood	甲 丙 戊 Yang Yang Yang Wood Fire Earth	庚 壬 戊 Yang Yang Yang Metal Water Earth

Since An Wang was born on a wood day, his wealth element is represented by earth. There is earth in his three known pillars of 未 Goat day, 寅 Tiger month and 申 Monkey year. There is also 戊 Yang Earth in the Heavenly Stem above his 寅 Tiger month. If we were to include his 丑 Ox hour of birth, there would be an additional earth element. The earth element is too plentiful in his chart.

When there are too many wealth stars in the chart, the person will not become wealthy. Instead, he will be struggling with money issues all his life.

He needed the 丙 Yang Fire which represented sun light to grow his wood. He also needed the 癸 Yin Water which represented rain water to nourish his wood. He had the 丙 Yang Fire in his 寅 Tiger month and the 癸 Yin Water in his 丑 Ox hour.

If he had all the necessary requirements, then why did he not succeed in business? He was intelligent and creative. He did well in his academic studies. He can have some achievement in life. Except that his achievements would not include becoming wealthy. He should have earned his living working as head of a design team or as a lecturer in the academic world. But he thought he was smart enough to go into business. He might be smart but intelligence was not the only ingredient for success in the business world.

His 寅Tiger month has a clash relationship with the 申Monkey year. The壬Yang Water in the 申Monkey clashed away the丙Yang Fire in the 寅Tiger. This clash caused his 丙Yang Fire was to become ineffectual.

His hour of birth was not known. However, he lived until 70 years old. There were certain key events in his old age that could help us deduce his probable hour of birth. He badly wanted his elder son to succeed him in the business. He was repeatedly advised by many of his senior managers that his son had no ability. But he tried very hard to ignore them and insisted on appointing his son as president.

Initially, the son did not want to join his father's company. But the father insisted so he had to comply. This meant that the relationship between them was not so harmonious. The father forced the son to do his bidding. Therefore, we deduce that the most likely hour of birth for the father was the丑Ox hour.

The 丑Ox hour has what is known as a bullying relationship with his未Goat day. The hour of birth represented, among other things, his children. In addition, his 未Goat day has a clash relationship with his 丑Ox hour. The water in the丑Ox clashed with the fire in the未Goat. This made his癸Yin Water useless. That was another reason why we deduce that his hour of birth was probably the丑 Ox hour.

THE SON

Fred Wang was born on a 庚Yang Metal 戌Dog day in the 酉 Rooster month. As the酉Rooster month represented mid-autumn, the metal element is at peak strength. There is also metal present in the戌Dog day and in the Heavenly Stem above the 寅Tiger year. If a person is a metal day master and the metal is extremely strong, it indicates that the person will be stubborn. In the case of Fred, he was not a bright person. The water element represented intelligence and creativity. There is no water in his known pillars of 戌 Dog day, 酉 Rooster month and 寅 Tiger year.

Fred Wang 12-9-1950

时 Hour?	日 Day	月 Month	年 Year
	庚 Yang Metal	乙 Yin Wood	庚 Yang Metal
	戌 Dog	酉 Rooster	寅 Tiger
	戊　　辛　　丁 Yang　Yin　Yin Earth　Metal　Fire	辛 Yin Metal	甲　　丙　　戊 Yang　Yang　Yang Wood　Fire　Earth

Once he made his decisions, he was not likely to change his mind. These traits were not conducive for the person who was appointed to head research and development. He was not flexible enough to respond to changes. He did not have an open mind to listen to ideas from other more creative people. When he was appointed president of the company, these weaknesses were exacerbated.

His 戌 Dog day of birth harmed his 酉 Rooster month of birth. The month of birth represented the parents' pillar. This meant that he would be likely to overspend or squander his parents' wealth. As he was a metal person, the mother was represented by earth and the father was represented by wood. There is 乙 Yin Wood in the Heavenly Stem above his 酉 Rooster month of birth. He liked and respected his father. But he did not have the ability required to manage a public listed company that employed some 32,000 workers. If he was given such immense responsibility, he would only lead the company to financial ruin.

His hour of birth is not known. It is not possible for us to deduce his hour of birth. During the tumultuous events in the company, he was only in his thirties. After his departure from the company at the age of 39, the public no longer had any reason to be interested in him.

THE EVENTS

On 23 August 1967, Wang Laboratories became a public listed company. This was the year of 丁 Yin Fire 未 Goat.

An Wang Luck Cycle

39	29			19			9
壬 Yang Water	辛 Yin Metal			庚 Yang Metal			己 Yin Earth
午 Horse	巳 Snake			辰 Dragon			卯 Rabbit
丁 己 Yin Yin Fire Earth	丙 Yang Fire	戊 Yang Earth	庚 Yang Metal	戊 Yang Earth	乙 Yin Wood	癸 Yin Water	乙 Yin Wood

79			69	59			49
丙 Yang Fire			乙 Yin Wood	甲 Yang Wood			癸 Yin Water
戌 Dog			酉 Rooster	申 Monkey			未 Goat
戊 辛 丁 Yang Yin Yin Earth Metal Fire			辛 Yin Metal	庚 壬 戊 Yang Yang Yang Metal Water Earth			己 丁 乙 Yin Yin Yin Earth Fire Wood

An Wang was then aged 47 and in his 壬 Yang Water 午 Horse luck cycle. There is no 丙 Yang Fire that he needed in the 午 Horse luck cycle. But the 午 Horse has a combination relationship with the 未 Goat year in 1967 and also with his 未 Goat day of birth that resulted in the fire element. This fire element was already strong in the 午 Horse luck cycle as the 午 Horse represented mid-summer when fire was at peak strength. When the午Horse met the two未 Goats, the strong fire was made even stronger.

His wealth is represented by earth. Since fire produced earth, when fire is strong, earth will be strong. He had the opportunity to make a lot of money during this period.

The best years for the company commenced from 1977 until 1981. 1977 was the year of 丁Yin Fire 巳Snake. As the巳Snake represented summer, the fire was very strong indeed in this year. The巳Snake also contained the 丙Yang Fire that An Wang needed. The company did very well this year. The Wang Word Processor had been rolled out in 1976 and the company basked in its strong sales.

On 4 October 1983, An Wang installed his son as head of research and development. This was the year of 癸Yin Water 亥Pig. An Wang was then aged 63 and in his 甲 Yang Wood 申Monkey luck cycle. Although there was the癸Yin Water that An Wang needed in the Heavenly Stem above the亥Pig year, the亥Pig had a combination with his 未Goat day of birth that resulted in the wood element.

Furthermore, the亥Pig year had a harm relationship with his 申Monkey luck cycle. The wood in the亥Pig harmed the metal in the申Monkey. To a wood male person, the son was represented by metal. Therefore, the issues that arose would concern the son. The son was appointed head of research and misapplied the company's resources such as manpower and technology. He did not perform well as the head of research. Instead, his key personnel who comprised the three chiefs of the design teams resigned. In October 1983, he publicly announced the launch of fourteen new products, none of which had even been designed yet.

As An Wang was born on a wood day, the wood element could represent Friends or Competitors. In this case, it represented competitors because IBM had mounted a strong challenge by launching the IBM PC. This product made the Wang PC and Wang Word Processor redundant. The company was left with their Wang VS minicomputer which had been launched in 1979 and was already obsolete.

On 13 July 1985, John Cunningham resigned. This was the year 1985 was the year of the 乙 Yin Wood 丑 Ox. The 丑 Ox year clashed with An Wang's 未 Goat day of birth. The metal in the 丑 Ox clashed with the wood in the 未 Goat. This could indicate that his Friend, John Cunningham, was unhappy over authority and power that had been granted to the son. The only viable option for Cunningham was to resign from the company he had served since 1969.

On 19 November 1986, An Wang appointed his son, Fred Wang, president of the company. This was the year of 丙 Yang Fire 寅 Tiger. The fire is said to be in the growth stage in the 寅 Tiger year. There is 丙 Yang Fire inside the 寅 Tiger. The 丙 Yang Fire represented authority and power to Fred Wang.

But the father, An Wang was then in his 申 Monkey luck cycle. The 申 Monkey clashed with his 寅 Tiger month of birth as well as the 寅 Tiger year. The metal in the 申 Monkey clashed with the wood in the two 寅 Tigers. This meant that the decision to appoint his son as president would not be a prudent move in the long term.

Against the Odds

Fred Wang Luck Cycle

40	30	20	10
己 Yin Earth	戊 Yang Earth	丁 Yin Fire	丙 Yang Fire
丑 Ox	子 Rat	亥 Pig	戌 Dog
己 癸 辛 Yin Earth · Yin Water · Yin Metal	癸 Yin Water	壬 甲 Yang Water · Yang Wood	戊 辛 丁 Yang Earth · Yin Metal · Yin Fire

80	70	60	50
癸 Yin Water	壬 Yang Water	辛 Yin Metal	庚 Yang Metal
巳 Snake	辰 Dragon	卯 Rabbit	寅 Tiger
丙 戊 庚 Yang Fire · Yang Earth · Yang Metal	戊 乙 癸 Yang Earth · Yin Wood · Yin Water	乙 Yin Wood	甲 丙 戊 Yang Wood · Yang Fire · Yang Earth

In any case, the reign of Fred Wang would not last long. On 4 August 1989, his father dismissed him as president of the company. This was the year of 己Yin Earth 巳Snake. Fred Wang was then aged 39 and in his luck cycle of 戊Yang Earth 子Rat. The巳Snake year represented summer. There was 丙Yang Fire inside the巳Snake year. If the丙Yang Fire represented authority to Fred Wang, then why was he dismissed during the巳Snake year? There was 己Yin Earth in the Heavenly Stem above the巳Snake year. There was already 戊Yang Earth inside the 巳Snake year. Since the 巳Snake year represented the summer season, the fire element was strong. Fire produced earth so when fire was strong, earth was also strong. In addition, there was also戊Yang Earth in the Heavenly Stem above his子Rat luck cycle. The presence of so much earth caused excessive earth to bury his metal day master.

If the son did not have the ability to manage a public listed company, it was the father who insisted on putting him in charge in the first place. It was tragic for both of them that events did not turn out for the better as hoped. However, it was not inevitable that a father and son team would drive a company down the drain.

Around that time, there was another father and son team in the American computer industry who feuded with each other. They were Thomas J Watson, Sr. and Thomas J Watson, Jr. Each of them held firm beliefs about how to run their company, IBM. By the late 1980s and early 1990s, "Big Blue" was already in trouble. But that is the tale for another day.